A
HISTORY
OF
METHODISM
IN
LANGLEY
a Cheshire Village.

Thelma Whiston.

The author

Thelma Whiston is a retired nurse who was born in Surrey. She lived in New Zealand for 6 years and Australia for 28 years. Much of this time was spent in New South Wales with her husband David and their children Jane, Paul and Elissa.

In 1992 Thelma and David moved to Macclesfield, David's home town.

The arrival of their three grandchildren, Karla, Tom and Pippa, during the 1990s encouraged Thelma to research the family's Whiston ancestors. This study led to an interest in the history of Langley, and subsequently to her agreement to write this book on behalf of the Members of Langley Methodist Church.

First Published 2003 by

Langley Methodist Church
Main Road Langley
Macclesfield
Cheshire
SK11 0BU

ISBN 0-9545008-0-6

Printed by Franklyn Publicity Macclesfield Cheshire

Contents

Acknowledgements

I have learned a great deal since accepting an invitation to write a brief guide to the Langley Methodist Chapel. The original, simple idea was developed to include a reference to the 300th anniversary of the birth of John Wesley. After researching the history of how Wesleyanism gained adherents in Macclesfield, and how and why it spread to Langley, the scope of the book expanded further.

Without the assistance of David Bullock this book would have been less comprehensive: "Thank You" David for reading the draft text, for your critical appraisal, and for providing much of the up-to-date information especially about the Church Organisation.

I also wish to thank Winifred Smith, MBE, for allowing me to have unlimited access to her personal papers and photographs relating to the Smith, Prichard and Moore families.

My thanks are extended to Miss Sybil Whiston for her memories of times past in Langley.

Mary Ashton, Philip and Dora Wardle, Keith Mason, Iain Smith and David and Heather Potts earn my special thanks for providing facts and pictures and their personal reminiscences of Langley, the Print Works and the Chapel.

Alan Chapman's contributions and practical assistance, especially with his expertise in the field of using his computer to set text and pictures on the pages, have been invaluable.

The late Cyril Dawson is duly acknowledged here for his pioneering publications about the history of Langley and its Chapels.

There are many other people who have loaned photographs, and others who have shared their knowledge of Langley, the Print Works and the Methodist Chapel: to all of them I offer my thanks and appreciation for their generosity.

Lastly, my thanks to my husband David for his support and suggestions – and for "word-processing" my manuscripts. If it hadn't been for his Langley ancestors I might not have tackled this particular history book.

Any mistakes and omissions, and the final choice of facts that have been included, are my responsibility.

Thelma Whiston,
Macclesfield.
March 2003.

Foreword

Where has Thelma Whiston been all these years? I would have valued having this book when I first came to be the Minister at Langley Chapel nine years ago! It is so helpful for a newly appointed minister to know something about the history of the building, and of those people who gather for worship and make the church.

We are about to celebrate 145 years since the opening of this present chapel, and a Methodist witness in Langley since 1794. This book is a welcome testimony to the lives of those who will make our celebrations possible.

John Wesley certainly made an impact on this part of "his Parish" and Thelma traces his involvement in the lives of those who were called to begin the Methodist movement in Macclesfield.

The building of Langley Chapel was also influenced by the Print Works and silk manufacturers in the village. Thelma describes how the village expanded by the building of terraced houses, with no inside WC. Many of the newcomers were Methodists, and from these people came the idea to build a new **WC** in their community.

In 1826 the first **W**esleyan **C**hapel was erected, and there is an interesting chapter on the construction of the building, and the formation of the church congregation. The Chapel flourished until competition in the form of Sutton St James' Anglican Church was built some 12 years later. It seems that many former Methodists then returned to their Anglican roots and the Chapel was doomed. Eventually the Chapel closed, and Methodists then soon began to meet over the village shop, until the present Chapel was built in 1858.

Thelma devotes much of the book to the expansion of the Methodist presence in Langley through the Chapel, and brings us right up to the present time.

Now, the village shop has gone, but the villagers continue to meet each week for "coffee and chat" in the Chapel. Thankfully, the old rivalry between Langley and St James has been replaced with a close bond of friendship and mutual support. Indeed, at the present time we are involved in talks for even closer unity.

The cottage industry and silk working have not survived. All that remains is the memory of those faithful souls who dedicated themselves to ensuring a real Christian presence in the village. This book by Thelma Whiston gives a remarkable insight into the dedication, commitment and self-sacrifice of loyal Christian men and women who have served their Lord in this place for well over 200 years. As the present Minister, I am proud to be able to say that the History of Methodism in Langley still appears to have many more chapters to be written at some future date. The Chapel continues to be a thriving and welcoming place of witness, care and Christian love, putting into practice the Gospel of Jesus Christ, and I am confident that 'A History of Methodism in Langley' will continue to be lived out for as long as there are people willing to share His Story.

Rev Derrick M Bannister

March 2003

Introduction

During the 17th century the Monarchs, Parliaments and the Church struggled, often against each other, to gain and hold power. Eventually various laws were enacted that were designed to force everyone to worship in the Anglican Church and to accept that Church's doctrines. Disobedience brought some very harsh penalties.

Until the era of the Wesley brothers and their associates, (and also of certain contemporaries of theirs), the established Church of England tended to treat the *"lower classes"* rather paternally. Generally manual labourers and the likes of servants, and also their families, were not taught to read and write. People such as these were expected to toil without complaining, and to obey the law and the rules of the Church without asking questions. Also these people were expected to be constantly dignified and sober.

Many in the property-owning, literate *"upper classes"* went to university where they studied subjects such as Latin, Greek, divinity, theology, philosophy, mathematics, medicine and law. The clergy were university graduates, as were many of the law-makers.

John Wesley differed from many clergyman in three important ways. Whereas some clergymen were anxious to lead genteel, sophisticated lives amongst *ladies and gentlemen* (rather than mix closely with the *working class*), Wesley wanted to communicate with everyone including those who actually produced grains, milk, meat, wool, fish, pottery, joinery, metalwares, coal, dressed stone and textiles – as well as soldiers, sailors and servants. Another of Wesley's unusual practices was to train lay people to preach and organise forms of worship that were readily accessible to everyone. The other difference to be noted here is that John Wesley was one of the first to promote the idea that everyone should be offered the chance to learn basic reading and writing skills: Wesley's followers organised some of the first schools for children and needy adults in areas where poverty was prevalent.

Maybe the established Church became worried about Wesleyanism and, in due course, with early Methodism. If the *lower classes* learned how to read, write and do simple sums they would soon begin to question – and then possibly disagree with – all that their *betters* had been preaching (under the protection of the law).

In 1874 the Rev. Thomas Hughes of St. James' Church, Sutton, expressed the view that the Langley Methodists were *"heretics"* because they conducted schools on the Sabbath. This opinion was far milder than the one that some other Anglicans had held only a few decades earlier: these clergy condoned, and sometimes even encouraged various forms of attack on the Wesleys and their assistants simply for offering to teach the poorer, labouring people to read and write.

Methodism did not set a "religious" course that was very different from the Anglican but it diverged from the Church of England largely on social and political grounds.

When travel was possible only on foot or by use of horses, Langley was linked more closely to Macclesfield than to any other place. The industrial revolution, with it's pioneering manufacturers and growing labour-force, and the Wesleys' teachings and ideas, became accepted and developed in Macclesfield before they spread to Langley. There was no place for worship either in or close to Langley before industrialisation spilled into that isolated rural hamlet.

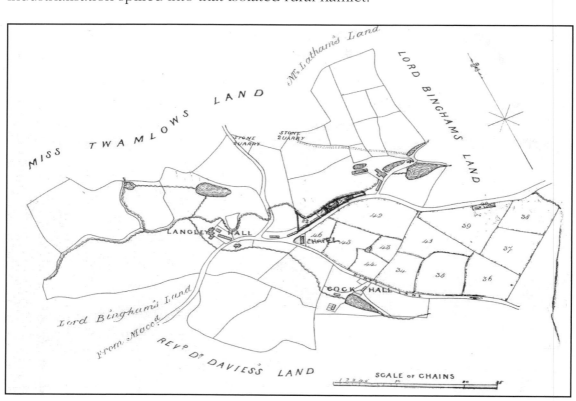

Langley Hall Estate c.1848

Langley Hall and its estate of about 220 acres had been in the ownership of the Clowes family since 1671. Around 1788 Charles Clowes, a cotton manufacturer, built a mill and some terraced cottages close to Langley Hall and near to the River Bollin.

Langley subsequently grew and, for nearly 150 years, thrived around a hand-block silk printing enterprise and the Methodist Chapel.

Whatever the religious views were of the small wares manufacturer and cotton bleacher Isaac Smith, and those held by William Smith of the Langley Print Works, there are many reasons to believe that they supported the development of Methodism in Langley and the Methodists' desire to build a Chapel.

When William Whiston inherited the Print Works in 1870 he also gave considerable support to Langley Methodists; he continued doing so until his death in 1915 although he remained an Anglican.

Apparently Methodism did not have much of a struggle to win religious hearts in Langley. The early employees in the textile works, drawn largely from agricultural occupations, clearly welcomed and benefited from the schooling provided by the Methodists.

In a number of cases three, and sometimes four, generations of Langley families worked in the Print Works and also worshipped in the Chapel. Their surnames include: Wardle, Downes, Steele, Davidson, Hooley and Dawson. Some individuals devoted more than fifty years of their lifetime to the cause of Methodism in Langley: included amongst these people are Samuel Ball, Cyril Dawson, Mrs Mary Alice Moore, Arthur Pickford, Wilfred Proctor, Mrs Ann Smith, Ralph Steele and William Whiston.

Aerial View of Langley c.1930

The history of Langley Methodists and their Chapels embraces three main phases. Firstly, the period from the late 18th century to the start of the First World War, which coincided with the *"Industrial Revolution"*, is when Langley changed from a rural hamlet to being the base of a major business, with a thriving Chapel. The second phase covers the years between WWI and 1964. The First World War forced many changes onto everybody including the Langley Print Works. Alternatives to hand block printing of luxury silks had to be evolved, and as a consequence many of the employees at the Works learned new skills. As the business became less profitable, the Chapel Trustees and fund-raisers also successfully faced many new challenges. The third phase bridges the era from 1964 to the present (2003).

When the long-term connections between learning, living, working and worshipping in Langley were broken finally in 1964, by the closure of "BWA" in Langley, the Chapel and the community were left to work together. Langley residents had to seek employment elsewhere – some commuted, and some moved away from Langley. Those who departed from the village were replaced by those who were able to commute to work outside the village, and by others who had retired. In spite of the significant financial, social and other changes, the Methodist Church in Langley not only survived but it has found fresh ways to attract worshippers and support while also providing new and relevant forms of "community service".

The interactions between, and the inter-dependence of, three important elements in Langley are included in this book. These elements are: the silk printing business; the general community in the village, and (John Wesley's) Methodism.

Langley Village Celebration c.1894

1

Methodism

"I look upon the whole world as my parish; thus far I mean that in whatever part of it I am, I judge it meet, right and my bounden duty to declare unto all that are willing to hear the glad tidings of salvation 'By grace are ye saved through Faith'."
John Wesley. (St. Mary's, Oxford. 11 June 1738.)

Methodism began in the early part of the 18th century as an evangelical movement within the Church of England.

In May 1738 John Wesley (1703 – 1791), already an ordained clergyman, underwent a "religious experience" that not only changed his life but also that of his brother Charles. Before his experience, John Wesley was a dissatisfied cleric in the Church of England, and afterwards he became a travelling evangelist who inspired an Evangelical Revival which swept the British Isles.

During the next 50 years John Wesley travelled mainly on horseback, but sometimes in a chaise, throughout the British Isles to preach at open air meetings, in private homes, in barns, and on rare occasions in churches, converting thousands of people.

Rev. John Wesley
1703 - 1791

As John Wesley preached his belief in the *"seriousness of life and earnestness of purpose"* Charles Wesley composed his uplifting hymns and together they brought a spiritual awareness to many people.

In the second half of the 18th century the Industrial Revolution caused radical social and political changes. Long-established social groups associated with rural life were transformed rapidly into urbanized commercial and manufacturing societies.

When addressing groups of believers John Wesley generally called them *"Brothers and Sisters in Christ …"*. The term "Brother" was then given to all the early itinerant preachers, and it is still used occasionally in Methodism some 300 years after Wesley's birth.

Taking the gospel message to the people, John Wesley awakened the conscience of those who had not been concerned with religion by stating -

"I ask not therefore of him with whom I would unite in love: Are you of my Church? My only question is this: 'Is thine heart right, as mine heart is with thy heart?' If it be, give me thy hand".

Rev. Charles Wesley
1707 - 1785

He believed in itinerant preachers and personal conversion, and also he proclaimed that education should be available to all: these were popular concepts with the working class but they were met with suspicion among the educated, ruling class.

A Macclesfield tailor, George Pearson (1718 – 1807), was converted in 1746 by Wesley, who then appointed him to lead the newly formed Macclesfield Methodist Society. This new Society, that started with five members including the leader, met in cottages to study the Bible and John Wesley's four books on the New Testament.

In 1771 the Macclesfield Preaching Circuit was formed so that Methodism could reach more people, no matter where they lived or worked. The itinerant preachers who lived within the Macclesfield Circuit were accepted readily during their rounds by those eager to hear the Gospel and the writings of John Wesley. (In the early days of Methodism the term *"itinerant preachers"* was used for those who extended Wesleyan ideas while making their rounds within defined circuits; later the title was changed to *"Local Preachers"*, which is the name used in this book.) The preachers' enthusiasm to spread the scriptures and their ability to relate to local communities helped Methodism to expand.

Before he was permitted to preach independently, each candidate preacher was required to undergo a six-month trial. Candidates had to be of good character, free from debt (be of independent means), and be able to read and write. Sound health was essential – because they needed to walk many miles, whatever the weather, often preaching at two rural venues in a day.

In Macclesfield the Methodist Society, which had grown in size, social status and wealth, built *"Wesley's Chapel"* in Sunderland Street, on a plot of land called *"Pickford Eyes"*, during 1779. The plot

Christ Church, Macclesfield c.1970

had been given by the Methodist John Ryle, (Mayor of Macclesfield in 1774), who also provided the funds to build the Chapel. One of the names on the Deeds of *"Wesley's Chapel"* is George Pearson, who had been converted 33 years earlier by John Wesley.

John Wesley visited Macclesfield on 27 occasions. Sometimes he preached in the open air, and sometimes in private cottages. Also he spoke at least seven times from the three-tiered pulpit in Christ Church, Macclesfield. (This Anglican Church, built by Charles Roe, was opened during 1775, when the vicar was the evangelical Rev. David Simpson). On at least three occasions John Wesley preached in *"Wesley's Chapel"* in Sunderland Street.

Wesley made his last visit to Macclesfield in 1790. A few months later, during March, 1791 he died in his London home. When John Wesley died he was still a member of the Anglican Church.

After his death The Wesleyan Methodist Church came into existence and -

> *"... the leadership passed to the Methodist Conference and instead of one person exercising leadership for a length of time, the President of the Conference became for the year of office the representative of the Conference and leading minister of the church.".*

Wesley's Chapel, Sunderland Street 1964 (with permission of Macclesfield Silk Museum Trust)

2

Early Methodism in Langley

Prior to 1826 there was no place of worship in Langley. In his book "Methodism in Macclesfield" published in 1895 the Rev. Benjamin Smith quotes the observation from an earlier era that *"Langley is beautifully situated but ungodly"*.

To attend the established Church in Macclesfield or Prestbury, villagers would have to travel along rough, often muddy, lanes and footpaths in all types of weather. For this reason members of poor agricultural households were deterred from attending church regularly. Generally they walked to church only to attend family baptisms, marriages and funerals.

The inclusion of Langley in the Macclesfield Preaching circuit in 1794 was welcomed and supported by local Methodists. Among the Langley Methodists at that time were: John & Mary Berrisford, James Bullock, Abraham Collier, Mathew Dawson, Peter & Esther Goostry, John Smith, Thomas Wardle, Ann Wardle, and Peter & Mary Wilshaw.

The circuit preaching plan of 1798 covered a large area. Within the area were 25 villages including: Leek, Buxton, Gawsworth, Prestbury, Rainow, Bollington, Macclesfield Forest and Langley. Later new circuits were formed when villages such as Leek and Buxton had grown into towns.

I.

A PLAN FOR THE MACCLESFIELD CIRCUIT.

1798-   1799.

PREACHING-PLACES.	HOURS	JULY 15	22	29	AUG 5	12	19	26	SEP 2	9	16	23	30	OCT 7	14	21	28	NOV 4	11	18	25	DEC 2	9	16	23	30	JAN 6	13	20
Macclesf'd Forest & Clough	10,2		7		11		17		3		5		10		16		18		15		6	12			15		17		16
Lower Eyres	8,5½	1	6	L	2	M	10		5	3	P	1	4	8	14		L	M	6	3	11	5		P	1		10		
Sithington & Withington	10,4	12				8		P		13		17		3		10		12		W		P	9		10		W		
Alderley Cross, etc.	1,3	P		6		3		17	7		P			12		5		10		17		10		10		12	P		
Langley & Gawsworth	10,4	9		3		7		10		9		6		17		3			7		12	10		17		9	P	3	
Broken Cross	3,7		3		4		9		7		12		17		12		10		9		5	7			17		3		10
Shrigley & Booth Green	9,1	10		8		5		4		6		13		15		9		11		10		13		5		6	15	6	
Bollington & Limah	9½	3		5	11		6		12		10			7		13		17		11		9		7		13	6		
Rainow	4	13		15	10		5		11		12		6	6		13		3		7		17		11		7	5		
Kettleshulme	12½,4	11		12	17		2		4		1B			9		6		5		18		1H		8		4	13		
Flatt & Whaley	10,4	8		4			6	13		15		11		10		8		8		18	16	11		4		?H	8		
Chinley & Chapel	9,1		2		10		13		6		2		1H	8		11			13		10	4		11			1H		8
Buxton	2,6⅓		4		3		6		13		10		8		11		2		14		4	5		6			13		2
Sparrow Pit & Tideswell	10,1½		18		19		4		10		8		13		6		16		18		2	19		13			6		1H
Edale	9,1		8		14		18		4		14		6	19		8		8		4		1H		8		14	14		4
Flagg & Chalmorton	10,1½	18		19		14		16		2		8		18		19		14		2		16		18		19	14		
Forest & Doveholes	12½,4	15		10	5		3		19		5		2	15		14		1H		8		18		4		19	14		
Prestbury	6	6		10	8		3		17		5		12	10		3		7		17		10		3			12		7

PREACHERS' NAMES.

1. GEO. SHADFORD.	5. JOHN GOODFELLOW.	9. JAMES LEAN.	13. GEORGE LOMAS.	17. JOHN BIRCHENALL.
2. JOHN BRANDRETH.	6. GEO BROCKLEHURST.	10. THOS. ALLEN.	14. JOHN TINKER.	18. JOSH. MYCOCK.
3. RALPH BURGESS.	7. RICHARD SALT.	11. WILLIAM BOOTHBY.	15. THOS. NEEDHAM.	19. ROBT. BURGESS.
4. JOHN GODDARD.	8. JAMES HARROP.	12. THOS. GREGORY.	16. SAMUEL BAGSHAW.	

APPENDIX.

Preaching Plan 1798

Two Ministers resided in Macclesfield and twenty Local Preachers looked after the needs of these villages. Preachers who had to travel more than six miles – for example from Buxton to Langley – could claim 2ᵈ (two pennies, or *"tuppence"*) a mile.

On alternate Sundays a visiting preacher held an out-door meeting in Langley at 10 a.m. – but if the weather was wet or cold the meeting would be in a barn or a cottage. After the morning service the preacher would probably walk to another village, such as Gawsworth, to conduct the 4 p.m. service.

In 1792, when Langley was still a hamlet, Mr Charles Clowes owned the Langley Hall Estate and he employed a few workers in his Langley based cotton bleaching business. Although most of the population of the Langley area was involved with rural activities, John Ball and James Bailey were already using hand looms in their cottages for weaving silk.

Langley Hall 1995

In 1806 the Langley Hall Estate was purchased by David Yates (1733 – 1812), when aged 73, a cotton bleacher and silk manufacturer from Manchester. In 1812 his son, also named David Yates (1761 – 1827), inherited the estate and moved into Langley Hall with his family. Although Anglicans, David Yates *"II"* and his family soon became involved with the local Methodists. In the words of the Rev. Benjamin Smith -

> *"God raised up a powerful friend in the person of David Yates Esq. – Mrs Yates was like-minded – they had the satisfaction of seeing their daughter Charlotte, especially zealous in the service of Christ, gather around her women and girls that they might learn the word of the Lord.".*

Another daughter, Susannah Yates, also taught the small group; later Susannah married the Local Preacher John Travis.

The gatherings conducted by the Yates' daughters were held close to Langley Hall in

Shippon at Langley Hall Farm 1983

a room above a shippon at Langley Hall Farm, reached by an outside stairway. In addition to religious instruction Charlotte and Susannah also taught the women and girls elementary reading and writing.

In 1815 a cotton bleacher and smallwares manufacturer arrived in Langley from Nottingham: this was Mr Isaac Smith (1781 – 1850) who was accompanied by his family and his nephews John Smith and William Morley. Isaac Smith rented *"Holehouse Cottage"* in Bollin Lane, and also a mill called the *"Bollinhead Mill"*, from David Yates *"II"*. Once settled, this Smith family (which was not Methodist) began a long period of helping Langley Methodists.

Four years later, in 1819, another manufacturer who arrived in Langley was William Smith (1785 – 1848) of Manchester (no relation to Isaac Smith), accompanied by his wife Harriet and their six children. William Smith rented parts of Langley Hall Estate from David Yates, and then established a small silk and calico processing business in some outbuildings near the Hall: his principle interest was printing with indigo dyes.

The businesses of both Isaac Smith and of William Smith expanded and, because of their need for more labour, extra houses were built in Langley. Most of the new dwellings were terraced, with two rooms upstairs and two down; there was no inside WC and the nearby river was the source of water for domestic needs. Many of the newcomers to the village were, or became, Methodists. They welcomed the decision made in 1822 that preachers should visit Langley every Sunday for services at 9 a.m. and 6 p.m., and on Mondays for prayer meetings. The times for the services were chosen to be outside the normal times of services conducted by the established Church.

In 1824 a provision shop and a smithy were opened, and a year later the *"St. Dunstan"* public house began business in the growing village.

In the Minutes of the Macclesfield Methodist Circuit, 1824, are the following names of preachers from Langley: John Travis, Samuel Ball, Joseph Chadwick, Robert Eaton, John Ball and William Morley.

Meetings held in the open and in cottages continued but in 1825 the Langley Methodists felt that the time was right to build a small chapel in their community.

3

The Wesleyan Chapel: 1826 – 1856

There's no reason to doubt that by 1826 the Langley businesses and the Methodists were already closely intertwined and moulded to one another. Close connections then developed between the silk printer and the Chapel, and these survived for 138 years – until the silk printing business in Langley was closed.

Even though they were not all Wesleyan Methodists, most of the Langley manufacturers and their families supported the proposal to build a Chapel – which was to include a Sunday School – partly because it would be beneficial for the work-people in the village.

Regular services in the open air, or in private cottages and barns, must have tested the enthusiasm of even the most ardent, pioneering Methodists. Probably because of the lack of shelter and a growing congregation, by the early 1820s the Methodists in Langley had begun to consider building a permanent Chapel in which they could worship, and advance the cause of their religion.

David Yates, who owned the Langley Hall Estate, generously leased a plot of land to the Methodists so they could establish a Chapel with a graveyard at the junction of Main Road, Langley Road and Cockhall Lane. The plot was roughly rectangular; on one plan the area is shown as 389 sq. yds. (In 1858 this original site was included in the site for the second Chapel.)

The Wesleyan Methodist Preachers Meeting in Macclesfield recorded in their Minutes for May 1825 that – *"Plans for a Chapel in Langley had been approved …"*

Walker Barn Chapel, probably similar to the first Langley Wesleyan Chapel

The Chapel Deeds indicate that the building was a simple oblong, which might have been aligned at right-angles to that of the present building. The specifications were for walls to be of brick or stone, the roof of slate or stone, and the timbers of either oak or pine. The specifications also called for windows in each side wall. Nothing is now known about the size of the structure, it's final details, the identity of the builder, or any of its costs, however the ground rent was £2/10/- (*two pounds, ten shillings*) per annum.

The Chapel opened for worship on 30th April, 1826. Brother Shaw of Macclesfield and two Langley Wesleyans, Samuel Ball and Thomas Goodwin, led the congregation in a Service of Thanksgiving.

Mrs Mary Alice Moore, a grand-daughter of Isaac & Elizabeth Smith, quoted details in a speech that -

> *"a choir of between twelve and fifteen members sat in two rows of seats in the "singing loft" adjacent to the wooden pulpit. A clarinet and a horn were played by Aaron Downes and Samuel Smith. Sometimes fiddle-players joined the other music-makers, and eventually a harmonium was installed in the Chapel."*

Local Preachers held Services each Sunday at 9 a.m. and 6 p.m.. Between these Services moveable wooden partitions were used to divide the Chapel into two classrooms so that children, and adults, could be taught reading, writing and scripture lessons. John Wesley's promotion of education for children and still-illiterate adults was well supported in Langley even though the established Church frowned on the Wesleyans for conducting schools on the Sabbath.

Mr Joseph Hine was the first Sunday School teacher. He was succeeded by Mr Joseph Chadwick who, in due course, became the teacher in the Chapel's Day School. In a letter dated 1898, Thomas Wardle observed that Mr Chadwick *"...was a very eccentric character from Macclesfield (but) as a school teacher he was very good indeed..."*.

Chapel pew rents were set according to each individual's ability to pay, but a few seats were provided free of rent. Worshippers were expected to contribute to collections each Sunday at the rate of 1ᵈ (*one penny*) a week and also to give 1ˢ/- (*one shilling*) each Quarter.

Some of the monies collected went to the Circuit Fund, and some were used to pay for maintenance of the Chapel building. Funds were also required for purchases of prayer and hymn books, for copy-books, for writing slates, and writing materials.

The Anglican mill-owner Isaac Smith clearly favoured the Langley Methodists' plans and actions: he became a major benefactor and his lead was followed in due course by some of his family. In 1838 Isaac Smith, soon after he had purchased the Langley Hall Estate from the Yates family, gave the Title of the Chapel and the plot of land to the Chapel Trustees.

The names of the Methodist Trustees on 19th May 1838 were –

> From Macclesfield: Joshua Thornley *Grocer*, James Sargent *Draper*, Thomas Brocklehurst *Shoemaker*, Finney Bower *Corn-factor*, David Holland *Silk Throwster*, John W Smallwood *Druggist*, John Clulow *Draper*.

From Sutton. Thomas Cooper *Farmer.*

From Langley. William Morley *Grocer.* Ralph Bailey *Grocer.*

From Meg Lane. John Smith Bailey *Farmer*, William Humphreys *Farmer.*

From Hurdsfield. John Boxall *Grocer.*

Langley men who preached in, or attended, the Chapel around 1838 included –

John Ball, James Bailey, James Redfern, Thomas Pymm, Thomas Wardle, John Shaw, John Holland and William Morley, as well as Isaac Smith himself.

The family-names of some of the other members of the Langley Chapel at the time were Ball, Cundiff, Dawson, Hesford, Sutton and Warren.

St. James' Church Sutton 1894

St. James' Church, Sutton Lane Ends.

In 1838 Anglicans in Sutton, and in some of its neighbouring hamlets including Langley, supported a plan to construct a Church in Sutton Lane Ends. Businessmen, including William Smith the silk-printer of Langley, donated money and materials. A number of farmers provided horses and carts to transport sand, wood and Tegg's Nose stone to the building site. The well-built St. James' Church was opened in 1840 by the Rev. William Hinson.

John Smith of Langley (1808 – 1870), a son of William and Harriet, was on the building committee and became a Trustee of Sutton St. James' Church – where both he and his father had family pews.

As the congregation of the new Church in Sutton Lane Ends grew, that of the Langley Chapel dwindled. The Macclesfield Methodist Circuit minute book records only 38 members for Langley in 1840 and of these some attended morning services in St. James' Church and evening services in Langley Chapel. The 1841 Census of Langley shows that there were 438 inhabitants in the village: the low figure of 38 members at about the same time probably masks the enthusiasm and energy of those who favoured the Methodist Chapel.

Langley from the 1840s to the 1850s.

Langley Methodists who continued to attend the Chapel and to support the Local Preachers during this time included: Joseph Chadwick, John Ball, Robert Eaton, Ralph Steele and Isaac Smith and his family.

Occasionally a Local Preacher missed his assignment: one entry in the Minute Book records that -

> *"... Bro. Goodwin was charged with neglecting an evening appointment at Langley because of the distance from Bollington, he returned to Macclesfield instead (and) sauntered around the town until 2 a.m. consuming rum; he disturbed a family in Brook Street and then woke the whole neighbourhood. His punishment was a three month suspension from preaching."*

A Macclesfield newspaper provided the following anecdote concerning William Whiston, about an event that occurred in the first Langley Chapel during the 1840s-

> *"When he was a little boy of five or six years of age, he was taken to the schoolroom, where a missionary meeting was being held, and he used a hat pin very indiscreetly and got a severe box on the ears for it, something he never forgot ..."*

Isaac Smith died of cholera in 1850; his wife Elizabeth had died in 1833. The loss of Isaac Smith's guidance and financial support might have been a reason why the future of the Chapel became uncertain. By the early 1850s fewer than thirty Methodists were attending Langley Chapel.

Without sufficient financial input, a contracting congregation, and with only fortnightly visits from Local Preachers, Langley Chapel faced the risk of closure.

Another blow to Langley Chapel around this time was when -

> *"Daniel Warren dropped dead during the singing of the first hymn at the Chapel. The Preacher, Dr. Birchenall, was so affected that he refused to preach from that pulpit again."*.

The Local Preacher Dr. John Birchenall, MRCS, was a devout Methodist and a medical doctor with a practice in Macclesfield.

An Act was passed in 1854 that amended the law relating to the certification and registration of Places of Religious Worship for Protestant Dissenters. On 15th February 1854 John W Smallwood, a Trustee of Langley Chapel, registered the Chapel as a place of Meeting for Wesleyan Methodists.

One of the last events in the chapel was in 1855. This was a "Tea Meeting" organised by John Smith as a welcome-home from the Crimean War for Sgt. J Wardle. He received a commemorative Bible from the work people and a gold watch from John Smith – who was now the owner of the Langley Print Works. The Chapel Choir was supported by Mr Haytor, Mr Hesford and Mr Holland, and Mr Moss sang to the piano accompaniment of Mr G Gee.

A year later, in 1856, the windows and the roof of the Chapel were damaged during a severe storm. Already by that time the floor and other parts of the building had been weakened by wood-rot.

The total cost for complete repairs would have been prohibitive; and also a debt of about £200 remained outstanding. The only realistic option was to demolish the Chapel building.

TO THE REGISTRAR GENERAL OF BIRTHS, DEATHS, AND MARRIAGES IN ENGLAND.

I the undersigned (ª) *John Wright Smallwood* ~~~~

of *Macclesfield* ~~~~

in the County of *Chester*, *Chemist & Druggist*.

Do hereby, under and by virtue of an Act passed in the sixteenth year of the Reign of Her present Majesty Queen Victoria, entitled "An Act to amend the law relating to the certifying and registering Places of Religious Worship of Protestant Dissenters," certifying that a certain Building known by the name of (ᵇ) *the Wesleyan Chapel*

situated at (ᶜ) *the Village of Langley in Sutton*

in the County aforesaid within the Superintendent Registrar's District of *Macclesfield* is

forthwith intended to be used, and will be forthwith used as a Place of Meeting for Religious Worship by a Congregation or Assembly of ~~Protestant Dissenters from the Church of England~~ of the Denomination called (ᵈ) *Wesleyan Methodist* ~~~~

And I request that this Certificate may be recorded in the General Register Office pursuant to the said Act. Dated this (ᵉ) *Fifteenth*

day of *February* 18 *54*.

John Wright Smallwood

(ᶠ) *Trustee* of the Place of Meeting above described

MEMORANDUM.—The foregoing Certificate was duly recorded in the General Register Office, this *Seventeenth* day of *February* 18 *54*, pursuant to the Act above-mentioned.

[signature]

Wesleyan Chapel Deed of Worship 1854

In order that existing Methodists were retained and new members recruited the next building would have to be larger, better constructed and more suitable than the original Chapel. Already, by the mid-19th century, the population of Langley was not only larger than it had been 25 years earlier but also it had become somewhat more prosperous and confident about the future with enhanced expectations.

4

Between Chapels: 1856 – 1858

The population of Langley continued to grow during the mid-19th century, due to the expansion of the textile processing businesses in the village. Around this period the Silk Printing Works was owned by John Smith, and the "smallwares" business was owned by Isaac Smith's son William Smith.

Between 1856 and 1858 there was no Wesleyan Chapel or Sunday School in Langley.

During these years Local Preachers held services every Sunday in a room above the provision shop owned by the devout Methodists Mr & Mrs Daniel Ball. Thomas Pymm and Thomas Wardle of Langley were two of the preachers. Many years later Mrs Mary Alice Moore recalled something of these services when she wrote that, as children, she and her sister-

> " … found the antics of the pigs in the sty under the back window of the shop were much more interesting than the lengthy sermons in which the grown-ups were engrossed."

Ball's Provision Shop c.1900

Efforts to raise money for a new Chapel began around the time when the first Chapel had to be closed. A Subscription Fund was started by (among others) two children of the late Isaac Smith. These siblings, who had become Methodists, were: Ann (by now the wife of William Prichard) and William Smith (who had married Jane Hine). Further support for a new building was given by members of the "other" Smith family – which was not Methodist – including John Smith, who in 1848 had succeeded his father William as owner of the silk printing business, and his wife Ann (*née* Whiston).

Benefactors of the Fund included: Mr William Smith, Mrs Jane Smith, Mrs Ann Prichard and Mr John Smith, who each gave 105 guineas; twelve ladies who gave a total of £60, and Langley village people who gave 5/-(*five shillings*) each. Other contributions were received from Methodist friends in Macclesfield and Bollington.

Years later Mary Alice Moore wrote about a fund raising expedition made by her mother, Mrs Ann Prichard, who was assisted by Mrs Jane Smith: these ladies called at a farm in Meg Lane for a donation and –

> *" the farmer offered them a calf if they were prepared to take it back to Langley with them. Mrs Prichard readily agreed the offer but Mrs Smith declined ..."*

William Smith
1825 - 1868

Jane Smith
1827 - 1915

Among their many fund raising activities the supporters organised a number of Bazaars and Sales of Work. The fund raising efforts were a great success: the debt of £200 on the first Chapel was cleared and almost all the money required to build the new Chapel, £1350, had been collected.

The second Chapel was built on the site of the first Chapel, which had been extended, and was opened in May 1858.

5

Methodist New Connexion Chapel: c.1856 – 1901

The Methodist New Connexion Church was formed in 1797 by a group of worshippers who felt dissatisfied with the way the Methodist Church was being governed. They wished laymen to have more say in church affairs and greater representation at the Methodist Conference.

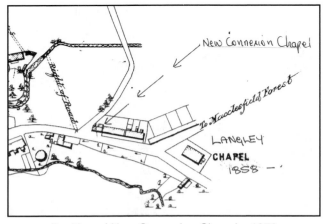

Position of New Connexion Chapel c.1870

Around 1856 a group of New Connexion Methodist worshippers built a Chapel in Langley, on the corner of Coalpit Lane and Langley Road, which they called "The Ebenezer" – sometimes spelt *"Ebeneza"*.

The little chapel, aligned to its adjacent terraced cottages, was built of stone and had an iron handrail.

James Hooley and James Hudson were the leaders of this Chapel. They both lived in Langley and worked at the Silk Print Works owned by John Smith.

The Ebenezer included a small school run by Mr Walker who taught reading, writing, and gave religious instruction to children and some adults. Education offered a brighter future for the children and the worshippers who at that time worked long hours for small wages. The Langley Board School did not open until 1878.

The congregation of The Ebenezer, which had never been large, had dwindled to just a few worshippers by 1891. This decline seems to have been a result of increasing financial burdens: upkeep of the little chapel was a constant problem. Income from pew rents was very low, and the Langley manufacturers supported the village's main Wesleyan Methodist Chapel.

The Ebenezer closed for regular worship in 1892.

Between 1892 and 1898 The Ebenezer building was rented to the Langley Wesleyan Methodists as an extension for their Sunday School.

The building collapsed in 1901 after heavy rains fell following a long, dry summer. An iron handrail that had adorned the steps outside The Ebenezer remained in place until 1987. The site of the former Ebenezer Chapel is now occupied by a conservatory extension to 63 Langley Road.

Handrail of demolished New Connexion Chapel 1901

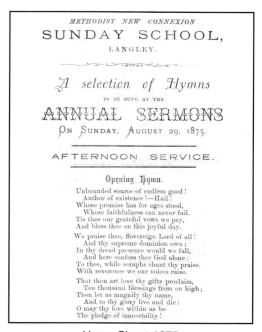

Hymn Sheet 1875

6

Langley Chapel: 1858 – 2003

1858 – 1908.

The well built new Wesleyan Methodist Chapel, large enough to seat 300 worshippers, was opened on Friday, 21ˢᵗ May 1858. It cost £1350 to construct. The site included that of the first Chapel but at 996 square yards it was more than two and a half times greater in area. The *"Macclesfield Courier"* gave the following details about the new building in a report during May 1858-

Langley Chapel c.1890

'The plans are by James Johnson of Macclesfield with input from Mr William Smith and Mr John Smith of Langley. Built of Tegg's Nose stone with Hollington stone dressings of early English style, the Church is substantial as well as beautiful. Above the door way, the Gothic window is filled with stained glass. The side windows, six on each side with stone mullions, are cemented into the stonework without lead or wood, to save on painting. Mr Hassall of Macclesfield carved the fourteen corbels of the windows .The gallery and pews are of pitch pine. The pulpit, less lofty than most, is of the same material. Care has been taken to ensure free ventilation, and heating is by hot water apparatus. There are tasteful gas lights. The east end of the building is divided by wooden partitions for the Sunday School and can be removed, allowing the children to join in the Service.'

The document of appointment of the new Trustees for Langley Chapel in 1857 records that the ground rent was £2/10/- per year (*two pounds, ten shillings*). The rent was paid to a member of the late Isaac Smith's family.

The land area for the second Chapel had been extended from the first site (389 sq. yards) by an extra 607 sq. yards to a total of 996 square yards. A notation on a contemporary site plan indicates that the additional 607 sq. yards was valued at £106. A well to supply water for *"domestic uses"* within the Chapel was situated close to the building: this remained in use until 1904.

The opening of the new Chapel was celebrated on 21st May 1858 with Special Services, held at 3 p.m. and at 7 p.m., when the Preacher was Rev. Samuel Coley of Manchester. The Preacher at the first Sunday Service in the Chapel, held on 23rd May 1858, was Rev. A. T. James of Huddersfield.

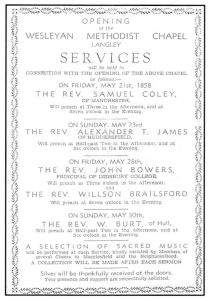

Order of Service 1858

Additional Special Services were held on 28th and 30th May when the Preachers were Rev. John Bowers of Didsbury College, Rev. Willson Brailsford and Rev. W. Burt, of Hull.

The Circuit Ministers at the time were The Rev. Willson Brailsford, Rev. Thomas Kent, Rev. Edward Jones and Rev. John Alexander Armstrong.

At each of the opening Services, Choirs from Macclesfield sang sacred music. The total collection from these Services amounted to £125.

Additional funds were raised for the new Chapel by way of celebratory tea parties organised by Mr & Mrs William Smith, Mr John Smith and Mrs Ann Prichard whose daughter Mary Alice wrote some years later about one of the first Services -

"… my mother Mrs Prichard and three other ladies were £5 plate holders. I sat with my two sisters behind my mother; my four year old sister Louisa started to cry and had to be lifted over the pew to sit with my mother.".

The Minute Book records that the Trustees in 1858 were- Langley residents: John Allen, John Bailey, Jos. L. Bailey, Ralph Steele, Thomas Wardle, and Jno Clulow; Macclesfield residents: Thomas Brocklehurst, Thomas Cooper, David Holland, James Sargent, and Jno W Smallwood; and *"of Meg Lane"*: Wm Humphreys. The office-holders were- Treasurer, and Minute Secretary: William Smith; and Chapel Keeper:– Samuel Ball (initially paid £5 per annum, but raised in 1859 to £6 p.a. to cover the cost of heating the Chapel).

The Trustees needed to encourage villagers (including lapsed Methodists and new members) to worship in the new Langley Chapel. To enhance the appeal of the Chapel they organised a number of new ventures

Bazaar Programme 1859

including Prayer Meetings, Tea Parties (to be held after special Services), and a Sunday School to teach children religious instruction, and basic reading and writing.

To clear the outstanding debt on the second Chapel, a Bazaar was held between 26th and 27th April 1859 in Macclesfield at the Wesleyan Centenary School. Many people, including Methodists and their friends, from Macclesfield, Langley, Bollington and elsewhere attended this successful two-day event. The overall profit realised on the numerous sales of *"useful and ornamental articles"* enabled the debt to be paid off.

Pew Rents. The Chapel's Minute Book for 1858 records that the pew Rents were –

Centre Family pews	10/- (*ten shillings*) per Quarter,
Side aisles, back	8/- (*eight shillings*) per Quarter,
Centre pews	7/6 (*seven shillings and six pence*) per Quarter,
Side aisles, front	6/- (*six shillings*) per Quarter,
eight rows at	1/6 (*one shilling and six pence*) per Quarter,
all the remainder at	1/3 (*one shilling and three pence*) each, per Quarter.

Pew holders were allowed to provide themselves with cushions, as long as these were coloured crimson. According to the Minute Book for 1862, William Smith and J. Bailey had to visit many local cottages and farms to collect pew rents that had not been paid.

Baptisms. The first baptism to be held in the new Chapel took place on 8th November 1858, when John and Elizabeth Shaw of Sutton brought their son William to be baptised.

The Whiston and Prichard link. In 1865 William Whiston, the nephew of the owner of the Print Works John Smith, married Emma Smith Prichard in St. Peter's Church, Prestbury.

William and Emma Whiston 1865

William was an Anglican and his parents, Charles and Sarah Whiston, had a pew in St. James's Church, Sutton. Emma's family was Methodist; she was a daughter of Ann and William Prichard. William and Emma had twelve children: seven were baptised as Anglicans in St. James' Church, Sutton, and five were baptised in Langley Chapel as Methodists. Emma's influence on her husband helped to ensure a secure financial future for Langley Chapel.

Treasurers. In 1868 William Smith the then Chapel Treasurer died, and his sister, Mrs William Prichard, became the next Treasurer. Mrs Prichard never allowed the Chapel to be in debt; her Financial Account for 1875 shows that the Chapel's income and out-goings for that year were –

Income		Expenses	
"In hand" (brought forward)	£50/15/4½	Lighting, Cleaning & Heating	£14/2/9
Pew Rents	£24/17/9	Repairs	£1/8/3
Donations	£8/14/2	Insurance (fire)	9/-
		Organist, & Choir	7/-
		Subs. to Wesley Fund	£1/1/-
		Paid to Circuit Board	£8/-/-
		Other Expenses	£1/7/-
Total Income	£89/7/3½	Total Expenses	£33/8/0
"In hand" (1875) (carried forward) :-	£55/19/3½	(fifty-five pounds, nineteen shillings and three-pence ha'-penny).	

Local Preachers. The Macclesfield Circuit Plan for 1880 shows that Local Preachers visited the new Chapel on Sundays at 2.30 p.m. and 6.00 p.m. for Worship and Sunday School Services, and on Mondays for an Evening Prayer Meeting at 7 p.m..

The visiting preachers were assisted at the weekly Prayer Meetings by Langley men including: Samuel Ball, Thomas Wardle and Ralph Steele.

Structural alterations.   By 1881 the Chapel needed some structural repairs, redecorations and the addition of a floor over the Long Room. These tasks cost £206/2/- (two hundred and six pounds, and two shillings).

Two other significant additions at this time were: the Gothic Arch containing the "Ten Commandments" board, presented by Mr & Mrs W I B Smith, and the *"handsome"* Rostrum (in place of the original pulpit) given by Mrs Jane Smith in memory of her husband William who had died in 1868 aged 42. Also Mrs William Whiston presented a font, made of brass with an inset silver bowl, which was used in the Chapel for many years.

A portion of the renovation costs was met by members of some Langley manufacturers' families including Mrs Ann Prichard, Mrs Jane Smith, Mr & Mrs William Whiston, Mrs William Smith, Mrs J T Moore, and Mr & Mrs W I B Smith.

After the renovations and alterations the Chapel was re-opened on Easter Sunday, April 17th, 1881, when the preacher was the former Circuit Minister Rev. John Eglington. At this time the Chapel Stewards were Joseph Steele and Mr John I Davidson.

Marriages. Langley Chapel was licensed for marriages in July1889 when the Superintendent Registrar was Mr J Frederick May. The Licence was *pursuant to the Acts 6th and 7th Wm. IV C 85."*

At the first marriage, held on 19th August 1889, Thomas Baldwin Worth, of Stourbridge, and Florence Smith Whiston, a daughter of William and Emma, became husband and wife. Mr Worth had a carpet manufacturing business, and was a second cousin of Stanley Baldwin.

Club activities. Rooms in the Chapel building were rented to various local groups. One of these was the Langley Sunday School Rambling Club, formed in 1886 when the membership list included:– Joseph Steele, F Millward, W Warren and William Downes.

This Club's Minute Book contains the following famous entry for March 1886 written by the Secretary, W Downes – without any "excuse" being offered (!) –

> "… that Members failed to appear [and so I] waited until 8pm.
> The Sec. proposed a vote of thanks to himself, which was carried
> unanimously, and he adjourned the meeting."

In 1896 the Langley Harriers Club was formed by William Hammond. This Club was based in the Chapel premises. Members of this Club went on to acquit themselves very well in sporting competitions. In his book "Langley – a History", 1988, Cyril Dawson quoted the observation that the best of these local athletes was, possibly, John Millward, a man *"… of small stature and yet one of the district's foremost harriers."*

Langley Harriers 1896

The Wesleyan Methodist Society.

Each branch of this Society was sub-divided into groups called "Classes". Each Class had twelve members, including a Leader. The role of the Leader was to support, advise and encourage everyone in the Class in their studies of the Christian beliefs and way of life that were fundamental to Methodism.

Between 1880 and 1894 a thriving Class met weekly in Langley. For the first eleven years the Leader was Ann Prichard, who was succeeded by Joseph Steele. Some members of this Class were: Hannah Shaw, Rosetta Davidson, Martha Lomas, Caroline Ball, Florence Bullock, Fred Millward, John T Needham, Ann Bailey and Hannah Parkinson.

Each member paid weekly ticket money of between 1d (*one penny*) and 5/- (*five shillings*) and they were also expected to contribute to the "Worn Out Ministers Fund". An entry in the Trustees' Minutes for 1913 shows that 10/6 (*ten shillings and six pence*) had been donated to this fund.

Extension for Sunday School. In 1896 a two-storey addition was built onto the Chapel, to accommodate the greatly increased membership of the Sunday School. William Whiston financed the new extension and his daughter Edith, and her committee, organised many sales of work to raise the money needed to pay for decorating and furnishing the new rooms.

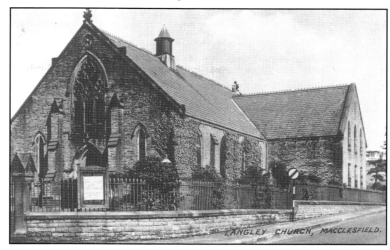

Langley Chapel with 1896 Extension

Chapel Keepers. Samuel Ball died in 1898: he had been the Keeper for more than 40 years. As the Chapel Keeper he had charge of the keys, and made sure that the interior was properly heated and lit before Services, and generally kept the premises welcoming for worshippers and other users of the premises.

The early Keepers dealt with a coke fuelled boiler and gas lighting. By contrast, in the more recent years oil- or gas-fuelled boilers have heated the building and the lighting has relied on electricity.

From 1898 the role of Chapel Keeper was taken on by William Warren. Initially he was paid £8 a year but in 1912 this was raised to an annual payment of £11.

Resident Minister. The arrival in 1899 of Rev. W B Alcock, Langley's first resident Minister, brought many changes to the Chapel. The members welcomed Rev. Alcock's guidance and support with the running of the Chapel and the Sunday School – which now had more than 150 scholars.

Rev. Alcock resided with Mr & Mrs S B Simpson in "Hall Cottages", Langley.

The Wesley Guild, formed by Rev. Alcock, was supported by many regular members of the Chapel.

Rev. W B Alcock and Chapel Members c.1902

<u>Piped water.</u> As the years passed, the old well in the Chapel grounds became polluted. To remedy the increasing health-hazard, in 1905 the Trustees asked William Whiston to grant them permission to connect the premises to his fresh water supply on Tegg's Nose. Mr Clayton, the builder, estimated that the cost for making the connection from the spring to a cistern in the school room and to the lavatory under the stairs, through a main pipe traversing Mr Whiston's field, would be £8: this estimate was accepted.

Horses and Waggonette
Outside Langley Chapel
c.1902

The result was that clean water was piped into the Chapel premises. As required by the Health Inspector, use of the well then ceased.

<u>1908 Anniversary.</u>

The 50th Jubilee of the second Langley Chapel was celebrated on 3rd May 1908 with a very well attended service conducted by Rev. W T Davidson, DD, of Richmond, Surrey.

Among the people who joined the festivities were Mrs

William Smith, Mrs M A Moore, William Whiston and Mrs Samuel Ball, who had all attended the opening of the Chapel in May 1858.

To coincide with the 50th Anniversary, the Chapel stewards Joseph Steele and Herbert Warren wrote a letter, dated Easter 1908, addressed to all the householders in Langley, announcing the start of the "Sovereign Fund". The following is an extract from the letter –

> *"There cannot be a family in this neighbourhood which has not been helped directly or indirectly as result of these fifty years of Christian ministry and that is why we do not hesitate to appeal to you to make May 3rd a record day in Langley's history.*
>
> *Signed –*

Joseph Steele, *Chapel Steward,*

Herbert Warren, *Chapel Steward,*

Fred Millward, *Society Steward,*

Harold W Whiston, *Society Steward."*

The purpose of the new fund was to raise £70 for the Chapel's Jubilee Sunday, to be called *"Thanksgiving Sunday"*.

1909 – 1964.

1911 extension.

Langley Chapel 1911 Sunday School Extension

A major addition was made to the Chapel premises in 1911. This was to provide more space for the Langley Wesleyan Sunday School. William Whiston paid for the building work and also he gifted an extra piece of land, having an area of 356 square yards, so that the total area of the Chapel site became about 1,352 square yards.

According to a plan, the 1911 extension had the nominal dimensions of 30-feet by 29-feet to encompass the new classroom, a kitchen and a basement.

The walls were built of stone brought from Tegg's Nose and Kerridge, and the builder was J. Clayton of Macclesfield – who had also built the 1881 and the 1896 extensions.

The foundation stone commemorates the Coronation of King George V on 22nd June 1911.

Mr William Whiston handed the Deeds to Joseph Steele who represented the Trustees. Mr Steele observed that the extra facilities would be a blessing to all the neighbourhood.

Activities in Langley were unusually lively on June 22 because a second ceremony was held that day. On this occasion a formal presentation was made on the corner of Langley Road and Coalpit Lane by William Whiston of his gift to the village of an extension to the Institute – now known as the Village Hall.

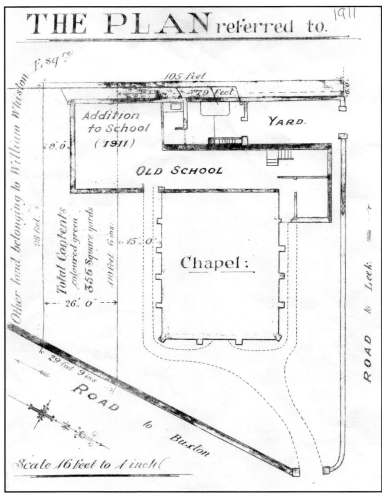

Plan of Chapel 1911

36

World War I.

Some of the more significant effects that the First World War had on the community, Print Works and Chapel in Langley were-

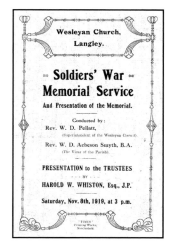

Memorial Service Sheet
1919

- demand for fine, printed silks fell, with grave economic consequences, and

- ninety-one village men joined the armed services, twelve of which lost their lives while serving their country.

During WWI members of the Chapel organised a Soldiers and Sailors Comforts Fund, which raised more than £150. The Chairman was Joseph Steele, the Treasurer was Neville Steele and the Secretary was James H Goodwin.

Lady members of the Fund knitted socks, scarves, helmets and gloves which were sent to members of the armed forces; Edith Whiston was in charge of the wool and knitted garments.

Times of the services held in Langley Chapel were changed, to mornings and afternoons, to comply with lighting restrictions enforced by war-time conditions – including the threat of air raids.

Insurance matters. The Minute Book has an entry for 11th February 1916 that refers to insurance matters, when the Chapel was valued at £3000. Cover could be extended for the first time to include damage caused by aircraft falling on the building.

In 2003 the Chapel premises were valued at £1 million.

Death of William Whiston. William Whiston died in 1915, aged 77 years. In his Will he left a legacy of £1500 for the benefit of the Chapel: the interest was to be used towards ministerial costs.

In spite of the efforts made by some of his children on behalf of Methodism, neither his son Harold nor the Print Works could continue to support the Chapel and Schools in the manner that William Whiston had done for fifty years, following his marriage to Emma Prichard.

Death of Mrs Jane Smith. Langley and the Chapel lost another long-term Methodist in 1915 when Mrs Jane Smith died. In 1857 she had donated 105-guineas (one hundred and ten pounds, five shillings) to the building of the Chapel, and between 1915 and 1936 her former home *"Bollin House"* was used as the manse.

Langley between the Wars.

The World War of 1914/18 changed social, commercial, political and religious ideas and practices virtually everywhere, including Langley. From the onset of WWI the demand for hand-block printed silks began to fall, and it never regained its Victorian-era popularity. Also from about 1914/15 Langley Methodists faced up to social, moral and economic challenges, including the loss of financial support from the printers and the owners' families that were entirely different to those encountered before WWI.

In the early 1920s the Chapel Stewards were Herbert Warren and Arthur Pickford.

The Stewards and the Trustees undertook further improvements in the Chapel including the installation of electric lighting, replacement of old ribbed window glass with fancy, leaded glass, and general redecoration. These improvements were completed before the 1923 Harvest Festival.

The Wesley Guild.

The Guild, originally formed in 1899, was reformed in 1923 for activities during winter months. The members included: Miss Edith Whiston, Herbert Warren, Arthur Pickford, Miss Louie Bay, John J Cragg, and John Manifold.

The pianist was Jim Simpson. The Devotional Secretary was Samuel Simpson. The Christian Service Secretary was Miss Gertrude Moore. The Social and Musical Secretary was Mr A W Dale. The Literary Secretary, later the title was changed to Cultural Secretary, was Miss Marion Broadhead.

The Guild continued with its meetings until 1938 when it was disbanded due to falling numbers and the prospects of a major war.

The Print Works.

Between 1915 and 1929 Harold Whiston introduced many innovative ideas to the Print Works. To help improve efficiency and safety, gas was replaced by electricity. To increase output and avoid total reliance on printing with hand blocks, screen-printing was introduced – as was printing on knitted fabrics. Under Harold Whiston's ownership, the Print Works acquired a fire engine to provide services within the Works' site and the village; the captain, Harry Dawson, and crew were men who worked in the Print Works.

Langley Print Works 1896

Also in this era a brass band was formed in the Print Works. By playing at Fetes and Sales of Work this band raised money for the Chapel. Also the band accompanied the Sunday School "walk of witness" around Langley village in 1929 and again in 1930.

The Print Works in Langley and many other established textile businesses were unable to return to pre-1914 conditions of production and profits, due to changed national and international commercial and technical conditions. In 1929 a number of textile specialist companies including *"J and T Brocklehurst"* of Macclesfield and *"William Whiston and Son"* of Langley joined together: a new company was formed under the name *"Brocklehurst Whiston Amalgamated Ltd."* (BWA). The Langley branch of the new BWA continued operating on the traditional site of the silk printing works.

Langley Print Works Band c.1920

Amalgamation of Methodist churches.

Early in the 20th century in Britain, the separate Methodist bodies began to coalesce. The Bible Christians, the Methodist New Connexion, and the United Methodist Free Churches united in 1907 to form the United Methodist Church, which in 1932 joined the Primitive Methodist and Wesleyan Methodist churches to bring the long chapter of Methodist disunity in Britain to an end. Today the Methodist Church in the United Kingdom has the distinction of being the "mother church" of world Methodism.

Despite the union in 1932, Macclesfield maintained two separate Circuits until 1950, hence the number on the current quarterly Plan (January – March 2003) is 213 - *see Appendix E.*

Langley Comforts Fund Whist Drive 1944

The Second World War.

Men and women from Langley were "called-up" for war service between 1938 and 1945. As in the First World War, the absence (and loss) of skilled, experienced workers and managers had a detrimental effect on enterprises such as silk printing. The silk printers had to change from their traditional luxury output – for which the market once again dried-up – to meeting the needs of the *"war effort"*, including the printing of escape maps on silk squares for use largely by airmen.

Records from WWII relate that members of the Chapel organised *"The Langley Comforts Fund"* to support the 48 local people who were serving in the armed forces. A total of 3721 postal orders and parcels were despatched. The committee for this active Fund consisted of: Arthur Pickford, Miss M Downes, Mr F R Garstang, Mrs Millward and Mr Rose.

Eisteddfod. The Macclesfield Methodist Circuit organised an Eisteddfod in 1948, for all the Methodist Churches in the Circuit. This included choral singing, elocution, recitation, sewing, embroidery, joinery and many other skills. Eisteddfods were then held annually for a number of years. Langley did well in 1948 and in 1949. Then twice, in 1950 and 1951, Langley won the overall Eisteddfod trophy. As one of the participants said in 1951 *"We sewed, cooked and sang our hearts out."*. The last Eisteddfod was held in 1970.

Eisteddfod 1951
Langley Chapel Winners
with Rev. Charles Somerscales

<u>1953 enhancements.</u> A renovation programme was undertaken in the Chapel during 1953. The re-opening Service on 19th December 1953 was led by Rev. C A Somerscales, who was assisted by Mr F L Freegard.

The Service was followed by a tea, held in the Sunday School. Mr J Blackshaw led community hymn singing in the Chapel, when Mr P J Connor was the organist.

<u>The Centenary Celebrations, 1958.</u>

Langley Chapel Centenary Tea Party 1958

The Centenary of the second Langley Chapel was celebrated from May 21st to May 25th 1958. Special Services were held, and entertainments, including Teas were organized.

Invitations to participate in the main Centenary Service were sent to all the surviving Ministers who had been resident in Langley. These five Ministers were:-

Rev. I Bond; Rev. A S Gregory; Rev. W H Noble; Rev. S Brinsley, and Rev. P Harris. (*The Rev. P Harris was unable to accept because of his advanced age and inability to travel the necessary distance.*)

The four ex-resident Ministers who helped to conduct the special Centenary Service were assisted by Pastor F G Crane and by Rev. C A Somerscales, who at the time was the Minister-in-Charge of Langley Chapel.

Langley Chapel Centenary
Silk Scarf 1958

As a commemoration of the Centenary, the local firm BWA designed a souvenir silk headsquare, on which views of Langley were printed.

And also exclusively for the Centenary celebrations for the Chapel, Mr Cyril H Dawson wrote his booklet entitled "Methodism in Langley, 1858 – 1958".

A special fund-raising offer was made of a BWA headsquare and a copy of Mr Dawson's booklet that together could be acquired for a single donation of seven shillings and six pence (7/6). Each donation helped the Chapel's finances.

In 1958 it was not realised that the Centenary celebrations would prove to be the last occasion when the village, the Print Works and the Chapel acted together. (BWA's Langley operation was closed in 1964.)

Closure of the Print Works. The closure of BWA in Langley during June 1964 was the end of an era that had spanned the previous 140 years, during which the Print Works, the local community and the Chapel had interacted positively and successfully with each other. The closure of the works resulted in 180 workers losing their jobs. Most of these men and women lived in Langley, and many had been employed in the Print Works for thirty years – and some individuals for as long as fifty years. A number of local families had been involved for at least half a century with both the Print Works and the Chapel, including members of the Downes, Hooley, Dawson, Pickering, Simpson, Wardle, Pickford, Bailey, Robinson and Millward families.

Arthur Pickford with Print Block c.1960

At the time of the closure there were many thousands of beautifully designed and skilfully crafted wooden blocks that had been used in the printing process. Possibly as many as 250,000 of these printing blocks were burned: most at the Print Works but some in fire-grates around the village. A few were sent to a museum in Italy and samples also found their way to the Silk Museum in Macclesfield.

1965 – 2003.

<u>United Services.</u> On 18ᵗʰ September 1965 the first annual United Service with St. James' Church, Sutton, was held. The Rev. Wesley Penny, the Methodist Minister, and Rev. Alan Stout, of St. James' Church, led the Harvest Festival Service in Langley. Later in the year Langley Methodists visited St. James' Church for a return United Service.

Joint Services continue to the present day (2003).

1975 Summer Fete Slideshow

<u>Summer Fetes.</u> The first Summer Fete was held in 1952, at the home of Mr & Mrs Mathew Barton, *"Brooklyn"*, Jarman Road, Sutton, in aid of Chapel funds. It was so successful that a Summer Fete was held in August each year until 1988. However, because unpredictable weather discouraged garden venues, in later years the Chapel premises were used to allow stalls and visitors to have some shelter when necessary.

First Summer Fete 1952
Rev. C Somerscales
and Visitors

In 1990 and 1991 the Fetes were in the form of cream teas and bring & buy sales. There have been no Summer Fetes since 1991.

<u>Trustees.</u> After being re-formed for the last time, the Trustees in 1974 were: Arthur Pickford, Robert Chadwick, Roy Cundiff, Cyril H Dawson, Wilfred Avery, Fred Collier, George P Naden, James Blackshaw, Mary Ashton, Alice Ann Millward, Philip R Wardle, Alice Baxendale, Elizabeth Barton, Claude C Harlington, Lily M Wilson,

David A Bullock, Pauline Manifold, George K Mason, Alan J Chapman, Katharine Barber, Eric Avery, Howard R Jackson and Rev. Albert Roebuck.

Church Council.

The Methodist Church introduced Church Councils in order to modernise the way in which individual churches were managed and maintained. The decision reflected changes that were occurring in society: many people were no longer working close to their homes, and it was becoming common for people to change their jobs and their place of residence quite frequently. Also some Trustees were now living in communities other than the ones in which their Chapels were located.

At the Church Council meeting held in Langley on 18th April 1977 the Rev. A Roebuck referred to the Methodist Church Act 1976 that had been passed in Parliament. This Act incorporated the dissolution of the local Trusts and their replacement by Church Councils as Managing Trustees, with the change-over taking effect on 16th April 1977.

It was agreed by all present at the Langley meeting that sincere thanks for the loyal service of all the members of the Trusts over the years should be recorded in the minutes.

Mr Pickford read the Minutes of the last meeting of the Trust, held on 30th September 1976, and these were duly signed.

Women's Meeting. A Women's Meeting met between the years 1947 and 1980. In the earlier years, weekly attendances peaked at 29. Attendances regularly exceeded twenty until 1960, when they began to decline.

Members of the Women's Meeting included: Miss Moore, 1947 – 1950; Mrs Whiston, 1951 – 1962, and Mrs Millward, 1947 – 1977.

Langley Chapel Women's Meeting Group 1934
with Rev. WH Willington

The Meeting ceased in September 1980, when only seven or eight ladies were attending each week. Members in the final years were: Mrs Blackshaw; Mrs B Barber; Mrs Goodwin; Mrs Downes; Mrs Hambleton; Mrs Redfern; Mrs Simpson, and Mrs Kitchen.

Mens Fellowship. The Mens Fellowship met during the autumn and winter months of the years 1954 – 1956. The President was Rev. C A Somerscales, the Minister in Charge of Langley, The Chairman was Mr H Baxendale, and the Secretary was Mr Arthur Pickford.

The Fellowship met once each fortnight, and the average attendance was about twenty men.   Guest speakers were invited, and in 1955/6 these were: Messrs Dickerson, Lamb, Howarth, Ellison, Ashness, Williams, Andrews, and Clifford Rathbone, Rev. C A Somerscales, and Rev. G Bassett. At one Fellowship meeting Paul Whiston spoke about his personal experiences of specialized military matters during WWII, and at another Sir Philip Brocklehurst gave an account of his journey to the South Pole.

The Fellowship Group. In 1970 The Fellowship Group of about twelve members was formed. The group met in private houses to discuss and enhance their faith. Usually each of these gatherings was led by one of the group, and on occasions the Minister also attended.

Since the mid-1990s the Fellowship Group has held joint meetings with Anglican members of St. James' Church, Sutton. Currently these joint groups meet in the home of Vic. and Janet Parkinson of Byrons Lane, Macclesfield – their house used to be named *"The Elms"*.

Prayer and Lent meetings. Since 2000 a small group of members has met for prayer on alternate Tuesday evenings in the vestry of Langley Chapel. The group is led by Tony and Jenny Lewis of *"Tolletts House"*, Sutton. Normally the Minister is not present.

Monthly ecumenical prayer meetings are held in turn at Langley Methodist Chapel, St. James' Anglican Church and St. Edwards' Catholic Church.

The three Churches also meet over a number of weeks during Lent to discuss relevant topics. In 2003 the topic was the proposed Covenant between the Methodist and Anglican Churches.

Youth work.   After a break of many years the Youth Club was restarted during 1970 on the Chapel premises.   Until 1977 it met each week on Tuesdays and on Sundays – after the evening Service.   In 1977 the Sunday meetings were changed.   The nightly subscription was originally 9ᵈ (*nine-pence*) and after decimalization in February 1971 it was 4p (four new pence) for everyone aged eleven or older.   To qualify for a Cheshire County Council grant, the Youth Club was "open", *i.e.* it was not restricted to those who attended Langley Chapel.   The peak attendance was 64 in 1978.

Youth Group before a Ramble over
Sutton Common c.1947

Between 1970 and 1986 some of the leaders of the Youth Club were:-

Eric Avery, David Bullock, Alan Chapman, Dora Dean, Wilf Dean, Norman Eardley, Jean Gosling, Maisie Smith, Jane Wardle, Sheila Wardle, Philip Wardle – *of the Langley Shop*, Michael Wilson, May Wilson and Helen Wilson.

Among the many activities organised for the club were table tennis, batington (miniature badminton), darts, snooker and listening to records.

Snacks and drinks were on sale. During a break half way through each evening, notices and an epilogue were read.

The Youth Club was closed in 1986 when nightly attendances were fewer than ten young people.

From March 1977 the Sunday night meetings were held in the homes of young members on a rota basis. For a time these Sunday meetings were held jointly with young people from Sutton St. James' Church, following the "Concourse" programme of discussions prepared in York by the Rev. Neil Capey, a former vicar from Sutton. The Sunday night meetings ceased in 1981.

Occasional special Youth Club events were arranged including: a sponsored walk – to part-fund the dry rot repairs in the Chapel; starve-in for charity; discos; collecting waste paper around the village, and attendance at national MAYC (Methodist Association of Youth Clubs) events in London and provincial towns including Coventry, Newcastle upon Tyne and Bath.

The following lines were written by a young person in the back of a subscription book for the Youth Club –

> *'In the parlour there were three*
>
> *He, the parlour lamp and she.*
>
> *Two is company, there is no doubt*
>
> *So the parlour lamp went out!!'*

<u>Coffee-and-Chat.</u> The Day School in Langley closed during 1970 – when the children were transferred to Hollinhey County Primary School, in Sutton Lane Ends. Then, in 1995, the shop and post office in Langley closed. Each closure further restricted the opportunities for local people to meet and talk informally. Mary Ashton (*née* Pickford) suggested, and it was agreed by the Church Council, that a mid-week social event should be held on Chapel premises to provide

Coffee and Chat 2003

an opportunity for villagers to meet. Mrs Ashton's idea has taken the form of a coffee and chat session in the schoolroom every Wednesday from 10.30 a.m. until noon.

The coffee-and-chat gatherings are well attended. Between 20 and 30 people are regulars and they always welcome visitors, including passing hikers. Donations given towards the costs of the refreshments are used for various purposes at the discretion of the organisers.

Among the regular visitors are Rev. E *"Taffy"* Davies, the Vicar of St. James' Church, Sutton, and Rev. Derrick Bannister, the Methodist Minister.

Some members of the Property Committee also attend this weekly function and take the opportunity to carry out repair and maintenance jobs while they are on the premises.

The Cheshire County Council Library Bus visits Langley twice each month and its arrival time coincides with coffee-and-chat meetings.

Each week a party of between eight and twelve of the people who met for morning coffee go on to the *"Leather's Smithy"* for lunch.

<u>*"Langley News"*</u>. Publication of a monthly newsletter called *"Langley News"* commenced in 1977. This is full of information about church events and other activities on Chapel premises. Included are the times when Services are held in Langley Chapel, and also the names of the office-holders.

Copies of *"Langley News"* are distributed free-of-charge to all homes in Langley. Free copies are also made available to members of St. James' Church, Sutton, and St. Edwards' Church, Macclesfield.

Issues of the weekly notice sheet provide further information about forthcoming events, and are distributed at Sunday morning and evening Services.

<u>Church flowers.</u> Flower displays regularly enhance Langley Chapel. There is a weekly rota of people to arrange the displays throughout the year. Some displays are prepared in memory of loved-ones who have died. Other special arrangements are presented by Church members for the annual Easter, Harvest Festival and Christmas Services. Special flower displays are provided by those getting married at Langley Chapel.

A flower festival was held in 1993, in conjunction with the appeal for a new organ.

Langley Chapel
Flower Festival
4th/5th/6th June
1993

Catalogue to the Flower arrangements

Friday	4th	June	10:00 am - 5:00 p.m.
Saturday	5th	June	10:00 am - 8:00 p.m.
Sunday	6th	June	2:00 p.m. - 6:30 p.m.

Proceeds in aid of ORGAN FUND
Flowers arranged by MACCLESFIELD FLOWER CLUB

Programme 50p   VALID 05 JUN 1993

Flower Festival
Programme 1993

Flower displays are not permitted in the Garden of Remembrance. Mourners can add their names to the weekly flower rota for the worship area, or may plant a shrub in the Chapel grounds.

At present the Church flowers are being organised by Mary McQuinn and Barbara Jones.

The Millennium.

Langley Millennium Plaque

A local committee including representatives of Langley Methodist Church made special arrangements to mark the Millennium 2000

The most important, long-term commemorative plan resulted in the erection of four unique, illustrated plaques: one each in Lyme Green, Higher Sutton, Sutton Lane Ends and Langley. The Langley plaque, situated in Tegsnose Mount, embodies an outline of the Methodist Chapel with a representation of the surrounding hills and trees, and the hand-block silk printing business that William Smith founded in 1826 is also depicted.

Reflections, early in 2003.

One hundred and seventy-seven years have passed since the first Wesleyan Chapel was built in Langley. The present Langley Chapel was opened 145 years ago.

Many children and adults have walked through the doors of the Chapels to pray, sing, receive instruction and share their beliefs – we will never know how many have done so since 1826. However history shows clearly that, since the earliest days, the Chapels have served Langley well.

The present Chapel is on firm foundations and continues to serve its members and the local community.

Langley Vision Statement.

To maintain a growing, caring and welcoming fellowship that develops spiritual growth and wholeness through worship and outreach to the community.

7

Church Organisation

The Methodist Church has its headquarters in London, where all the central business is controlled and transacted, with the main exception of property matters which is based in Manchester. The office for The Methodist Publishing House is in Peterborough, and Derby is the location of the Methodist Homes' office.

The national Methodist Conference meets in a different venue each year, under the chairmanship of the President. All major decisions concerning the Church are taken at the annual Conference. Delegates at the Conference elect the Church President, who is a Methodist Minister and who serves for one year only. Also, a lay person is elected each year as the Vice-President.

Below national level the Methodist Church is divided into 33 Districts. The Chairmen for the Districts are appointed by the Conference from amongst Methodist Ministers; the position of Chairman is paid and permanent.

Districts are sub-divided into Circuits. Each Circuit has a number of appointed Ministers. Initially each appointment is for between three and five years, however terms can be extended by joint agreement between the Minister and the Circuit. Methodist Ministers take up their new appointment on 1st September.

Langley Chapel is in the Macclesfield Circuit, one of 22 within the Manchester and Stockport District.

In 2003 Macclesfield Circuit has three Ministers who have responsibility for ten Churches and 579 members. The Circuit is administered by three Circuit Stewards: presently one of them, Tony Lewis, is a member at Langley.

Four Supernumerary (Retired) Ministers presently live in the Macclesfield Circuit. They undertake various roles including the responsibility for a smaller Chapel, and filling-in for full-time Ministers during periods of sickness and sabbatical leave.

Since 1974 local Methodist Churches, including Langley, have been governed by Church Councils which work within National, District and Circuit guidelines. Church Councils replaced the former Leaders Meetings and Trustees. In order to expedite the work of the local Church, Langley has appointed several committees to handle matters concerning: Worship; Mission; Pastoral; Property; Budget, and Young People – *see Appendix D*.

Church Stewards.

Over the years Church Stewards have been appointed to ensure that the Church runs smoothly. A Senior Steward is appointed from one of their number.

Some of those who have been Stewards in Langley since 1862 are -

1862	William Smith *(son of Isaac Smith)*
1881	Ralph Steele
1890	Joseph Steele, and John I Davidson
1908	Joseph Steele, and Herbert Warren
1920	Herbert Warren, and Arthur Pickford
1950	Arthur Pickford, and Percy Naden
1992	Dora Dean (*née* Barber), Derek Lockett, Andrew Green, Tony Lewis, Roger Preston and David Bullock.
2001	Derek Lockett, David Bullock, Brenda Chapman, David Potts, Dennis Sitch and Jenny Lewis.

Joseph & Harriet Steele, sons John & Neville with Mrs Ann Smith 1890

Church Treasurer.

The role of Treasurer has always been important: the bearer of this office has to ensure that the church is able to meet its financial commitments. In Langley, over the years this position has been filled by many worthy people, including -

From	Treasurer	Up to
1858	William Smith	1868
1868	Mrs Ann Prichard	1891
1891	William Whiston	1915
1915	Wm Hartington Whiston	1928 ?
1957	Walter Bloor	1970
1970	Percy Naden	1992
1992	Philip Wardle	

Church Secretary.

In addition to taking the minutes of meetings, the Church Secretary has the important task of pursuing matters agreed at those meetings.

Until the mid-1970s the secretarial tasks were divided amongst the various administrative groups such as the Trust, the Ministerial Fund, and the Leaders Meeting. Following the inception of Church Councils in 1974 and the dissolution of the Trusts in 1976 the separate secretarial duties have been amalgamated. Since those changes the holders of this office in Langley have been -

From	Church Secretary	Up to
1974	Philip Wardle	1979
1979	Mary Ashton (*née* Pickford)	1992
1992	Alan Chapman	

Church membership. The Methodist Church maintains an official Membership list, which is formalised through a church service of reception. Some membership statistics for recent decades are-

Year	Langley	Macclesfield Circuit
1985	55	
1986	67	769
1990	66	
2003	78 *and 63 adherents*	579

In addition to new members joining directly in Langley others have joined by transferring to Langley – often after moving into the locality, or after their own Methodist Chapels have closed – for example, after the closures of: The Ebenezer, Langley; Meg Lane, Sutton; Hollin Lane, Sutton; Brunswick, Macclesfield; Stamford Road, Macclesfield, and Allgreave, Wildboarclough.

1996 Safari Lunch, Main Road
Alan Chapman, Bessie Wardle,
Cyril Dawson, Heather Potts,
Brenda Chapman, Elsie Hammond

The number of members in 2003 is 78, the highest level for many years. In addition there are some people who are not members but have an association with Langley Chapel and they are known as "adherents": in 2003 there were 63 adherents.

Attendance at the 10.30 a.m. Sunday Services, including children and young people, reflects but rarely exceeds the membership total of 78. The 6.30 p.m. Sunday Services usually attract about 15 adults, but no children. Attendances at the Junior Church (the "Sunday Club") fluctuate between none and eight.

In 2003 few of the congregation arrive on foot, most travel by car (there is no bus service to Langley on Sundays). The choice of car travel reflects the fact that most of those who now worship in Langley Chapel live outside the village.

The lists of office holders and membership of the church council and committees in *Appendix D* give an indication of the broad range of work undertaken by church members.

Finances.

In 2003 the finances of Langley Methodist Church are recorded under two main headings; the General Account, and the Property Account.

Both of these accounts are under the control of the Church Council which also has control of a separate fund known as the Remembrance Fund, the proceeds of which are for the upkeep and improvement of the Chapel premises.

Income from the letting of the premises, and from the sale of memorial stones in the Garden of Remembrance, are credited to the Property Account. All other income is credited to the General Account.

The main expenditure from the General Account is the Circuit Assessment. This is to pay largely for the Ministers' salaries and the running expenses of the manses. Donations are also made from the General Account for charitable purposes. Any surplus on the General Account is transferred to the Property Account.

The Property Account is used to pay for the running costs of the premises, including repairs and improvements. Any shortfall on the Property Account is met by transfer from the Remembrance Fund.

The Budget Committee and the Property Committee make recommendations to the Church Council about administration of the church's finances.

In addition to the above, numerous additional purposes are accounted for separately; these include-

Methodist organisations -

Choir.
Home, and Overseas, Missions.
JMA (Junior Mission for All).
Junior Church (previously "Sunday School"), also known as The Sunday Club.
Methodist Homes (MHA).
Methodist Relief and Development Fund (MRDF).
NCH, formerly National Childrens Homes.
Sunday and Wednesday refreshments, including the Coffee & Chat group.
Womens Network.

Non-Methodist organisations -

Christian Aid, and
Tearfund sponsorship.

Historically the following purposes were accounted for separately -

Trust Account, 1858 – 1997.
Ministerial Fund, 1907 – 1959.
Poor Fund.
Retired Ministers and Widows Fund.
Ministers' Benevolent Fund.
General Chapel Fund.

Youth Club.

Wesley Guild.

Mens Fellowship, 1954 – 1956.

Class Money.

Jumble Sale Committee, 1920 – 1935.

Missionary Account, 1929 – 1947.

The main sources of regular income to the church are: the Envelope System; the Remembrance Fund, and Gift Aid (tax refund). Thanks to the generous giving by church members, and substantial receipts from legacies by former members, the financial position of Langley Methodist Church is very sound.

Langley Chapel Trip to Southport 1933
Minister – Rev. W H Willington

Therefore fund raising *via* concerts, sales and other special events can now concentrate on the charitable projects supported by Church members.

Use of the premises.

In addition to the Sunday Services and other Church-sponsored meetings, the Langley Chapel premises are also used on a regular basis by –

Yoga classes	Monday afternoon.
Table tennis club	Monday evening.
Cheshire County Council Day Care for the Elderly	Tuesday and Thursday.
Scottish dancing (adults)	Tuesday evening.
Coffee & Chat for local community	Wednesday morning.
Bridge class	Wednesday afternoon.
Choir practice	Thursday evening.
U3A (University of the Third Age) painting group	Two Fridays each month.
Scottish dancing (children)	Saturday morning.

Other lettings occur from time to time for: birthday parties; the home watch group; Sutton Womens Institute; Sutton Parish Council, and for band practices.

8

Methodist Ministers

The four Circuit Ministers in 1887 are shown in the photograph. They were: back row left to right Rev. Benjamin Smith, Superintendent and author of "Methodism in Macclesfield" 1895, Rev. J Norton, and front row Rev. J Parkyn and Rev. W. W. Spencer. Until 1899 Methodist Ministers and Local Preachers visited Langley Chapel each Sunday at 2.30 p.m. and 6 p.m. for services and on Mondays at 7 p.m. to hold prayer meetings. There were also special services such as baptisms and marriages.

Circuit Ministers 1887

The growth of the Chapel's congregation and of the Sunday School's membership encouraged the Trustees to make a request to the Macclesfield Wesleyan Quarterly Circuit Meeting for a resident Minister in Langley. This request was granted on the condition that the congregation raised enough money to pay for and cover all the costs of a resident Minister during the following eight years. After months of fundraising, the money was raised and in 1899 Rev. W B Alcock was appointed the first resident Minister in Langley; he resided with Mr & Mrs S B Simpson in *"Hall Cottages"*, Langley.

Under the Rev. Alcock's guidance membership of both the Chapel and the Sunday School increased. Mr Alcock formed The Wesley Guild, an initiative that was enthusiastically welcomed. The Guild's first meeting, on 17th October 1899, was attended by Harold Whiston, John Thomas Moore, Mr H Warren, Mr J I Davidson, Fred Millward, Miss Marie Dawson, Joseph Steele, John Avery and Rev. W Alcock. The Sunday School was represented at this meeting by Thomas Wardle, William Hammond and Miss Gertrude Moore.

Members of The Guild acknowledged their responsibilities to the community and to the Chapel, and also they worked as a group to enhance devotional, cultural, social and missionary service.

After three years, in August 1902, the Rev. Alcock was transferred from the village to a post in South Africa – the move was regretted by all in Langley.

On a Saturday shortly before the departure of Rev. Alcock, a commemorative photograph was taken outside Langley Hall (by Mr Bullock, the Macclesfield photographer) of the Minister with members of the Langley Methodist Chapel. After posing for the photograph the whole group made their way in waggonettes and on bicycles to Rudyard Lake, where they had a picnic.

On the Sunday following the picnic a farewell service was held in the Chapel at which the large congregation was attentive, sympathetic and somewhat tearful. The Rev. Alcock observed that all the Wesleyan traditions had become very strongly embraced in the Langley area before his arrival. Mr Alcock also stated that the Langley *"... sphere was peculiar: one of the smallest and most compact in the country".* For these reasons Rev. Alcock had come to know all his people intimately *" ... as brothers and sisters, friends in Jesus Christ"* and felt that he had been more like a Church vicar than a Methodist preacher in Langley. In Lancashire his work had been hard and solitary, but while in Langley he had not needed to struggle with the task of converting people to Methodism but was able to work with and for the majority of villagers because they were active Methodists already. Rev. Alcock gave thanks to the wives, sisters and mothers in Langley but he added *"our hearts have yearned for the husbands, brothers and sons"* who attended Chapel more for amusement than for Christian profit and worship.

In 1904 William Whiston built *"Invercraig"* as a wedding present for his youngest son Hartington. Adjoining this house was an extension called "The Manse" – later renamed *"Abbotsdale"*. The Rev. G H Bamford was the first occupant of the new manse in 1904; it served as the Langley residence for Methodist Ministers until 1915.

After the death in 1915 of Mrs Jane Smith, her residence *"Bollin House"* (on the corner of *Main Road* and

'Invercraig' and 'The Manse'
Eric and Sybil Whiston 1911

Holehouse Lane, Langley) became the manse. Resident Methodist Ministers lived in the Bollin House manse until 1939. This property was sold in 1940 by the owner Harold Whiston.

During the Second World War the Ministers lived in private homes in Langley. By the end of WWII the Chapel's congregation had dwindled and many of its benefactors had died. After the departure from Langley in 1945 of Pastor T D Till, the reduced congregation, working alone, could not continue to meet the costs of supporting a resident Minister.

From 1946 the Langley Chapel was served by Ministers who lived in Macclesfield. These Ministers also looked after a number of other Chapels in the area.

<u>1958:</u> Before the Centenary of the Langley Chapel, invitations to participate in the main Service were sent to all the surviving Ministers who had been resident in

1958 Centenary Celebrations

Langley. The Rev. Isaac Bond, Rev. A S Gregory, Rev. W H Noble and Rev. S Brinsley accepted but Rev. H Percival Harris was unable to do so due to his advanced years.

The Centenary Celebrations were held between May 21st and May 25th, 1958.

The four ex-resident Ministers who returned to conduct the special Centenary Service were assisted by Pastor F G Crane and by the Minister in Charge of Langley Chapel, the Rev. C A Somerscales.

Summer Fete 1971 with Sister Joy Hale

In 1969 Sister Phyllis Osborne was appointed as the first Deaconess to serve at Langley. She was followed in 1970 by Sister Joy Hale, who was the first woman to conduct a burial service, and also the first to conduct a marriage service, in Langley Chapel. Sister Hale went on to become one of the first women ordained Ministers in the Methodist Church.

Local Preachers.

The Methodist Church has always relied heavily on lay preachers for the conduct of many of its services of public worship. These are currently known as Local Preachers. Persons putting themselves forward for training as a Local Preacher must be accepted by the Circuit's Local Preachers' Meeting. They then go *"on note"* for a period before advancing to the stage of *"on trial"*. After a period of theoretical and practical training (including examinations) they are accepted onto the Plan as fully accredited Local Preachers, normally *via a* Service of Welcome at Circuit level.

In early 2003 the Macclesfield Circuit consisted of –

- three Ministers: Rev. Mark Broadhurst (Superintendent), Rev. Derrick Bannister, and Rev. Ruth Jackson;
- sixteen accredited Local Preachers (plus three on trial);
- one candidate studying for the ministry, Mrs Jocelyn Bennett, and
- three Circuit Stewards.

In addition to the Ministers and Local Preachers on the Circuit list, the Superintendent Minister of the Circuit can also call on accredited preachers from other Circuits (known as *"Visiting Preachers"*) in order to meet the demand for preaching appointments in the Circuit, or to preach at special services such as Chapel anniversaries.

Macclesfield Methodist Ministers who officiated at Langley, 1858 – 1898.

1858	Rev. Willson Brailsford (Baptism)
1859	Rev. Edward Jones (B), *and* Rev. John Alexander Armstrong (B)
1861	Rev. William Hurst (B), *and* Rev. Alfred I French (B)
1862	Rev. R Williams (B)
1863	Rev. J J Wray (B)
1864	Rev. John G Cox (B)
1867	Rev. George Scott (B), *and* Rev. Samuel Wilkinson (B)
1870	Rev. Jas. Nicholson (B)
1871	Rev. John Eglinton (B)
1873	Rev. Joseph Adams (B), *and* Rev. Michael Johnson (B)
1876	Rev. Thomas Asbourn (B), *and* Rev. John Rhodes (B)
1878	Rev. A Percy Watson (B)
1879	Rev. M Barker (B), *and* Rev. John Hootson (B)
1881	Rev. Richard Middleton (B)
1882	Rev. J Bampton Maltby (B)
1884	Rev. J Dodsworth (B)
1886	Rev. Benjamin Smith (B), *and* Rev. Joseph Baker Norton (B)
1887	Rev. W Woodward Spencer (B)
1889	Rev. Fred. Hughes (B), *and* Rev. William Wilson (Marriage)
1891	Rev. Frederick Elton (M), *and* Rev. Thomas McCullogh (M)
1892	Rev. Edwin Coulson (B)
1894	Rev. W Percy Hutton (B)
1896	Rev. S I Howard (B), *and* Rev. I H Clemenson (B)
1898	Rev. Edward Brentnall (M)

Ministers from Langley.

The following men who were born in Langley were ordained into the Methodist ministry: Rev. George A Parkinson, 1905; Rev. William Parkinson, 1910; Rev. James Simpson, 1920, and Rev. Clifford Sutton, 1941.

Langley Ministers: 1899 – 2003.

Appointed	Minister	Residence, & etc
1899	Rev. W B ALCOCK	First Resident minister in Langley. Resided with Mr & Mrs S B Simpson, *Hall Cottages*, Langley
1902	Rev. E Elam GREAVES	with: Mr & Mrs S B Simpson, *Hall Cottages*.
1904	Rev. G H BAMFORD	The Manse, adjoining *"Invercraig"*
1905	Rev. W E CULLWICK	Rev. Cullwick supplied when Rev. Bamford was ill.
1907	Rev. H Percival HARRIS	The Manse, next to *Invercraig*, Langley
1910	Rev. Arthur PHILLIPS	The Manse, next to *Invercraig*, Langley
1913	Rev. H W SLADER	The Manse, next to *Invercraig*, Langley
1917	Rev. Frederick HUGHES	The Manse (was *"Bollin House"*), Langley
1919/1924	*No resident Ministers in Langley*	
1919	Rev. Walter FYTCHE	lived in Macclesfield
1922	Rev. R T MORRISON	lived in Macclesfield
1924	Rev. W H NOBLE	The Manse (was *"Bollin House"*), Langley.
1927	Rev. A S GREGORY	The Manse (was *"Bollin House"*), Langley..
1930	Rev. Isaac BOND	The Manse (was *"Bollin House"*), Langley..
1933	Rev. W H WILLINGTON	The Manse (was *"Bollin House"*), Langley
1936	Rev. F E DAVIES	The Manse (was *"Bollin House"*), Langley
1939/1940	Rev. T A SIMPSON,	from The Wesleyan Chapel, Macclesfield.
1940	Rev. H Sheridan BRINSLEY	with: Mr & Mrs C Downes, Langley Hall, *then after his marriage* in Main Road, Langley.
1943	Rev. James BUTLER	with: the Bolshaw family, Clarke Lane Farm, Langley.
1945	Pastor T D TILL	with: the Misses Warren, Langley Road. The last resident Minister in Langley.
1946	Pastor F G CRANE	Lyme Green, Sutton.
1949	Rev. J E GRIFFITHS	Lyme Green, Sutton.
1950	Rev. C A SOMERSCALES	Fernley Manse, Fence Avenue, Macclesfield.
1958	Rev. Bernard HOLLAND	Fernley Manse, Fence Avenue, Macclesfield.
1962	Rev. Wesley U PENNEY	Fernley Manse, Fence Avenue, Macclesfield.
1967	Rev. Leslie J HEWITT	The Manse, Buxton Road, Macclesfield.
1968	Rev. Ralph W DALE	The Manse, Gawsworth Road, Macclesfield.
1969	Sister Phyllis OSBORNE	Westminster Road Flats
1970	Sister Joy HALE	Victoria Park Flats
1973	Rev. Albert ROEBUCK	The Manse, Lyme Avenue, Macclesfield
1981	Rev. E Ann BUCKROYD	The Manse, Lyme Avenue, Macclesfield
1984	Rev. Alan L ASHLEY	The Manse, Lyme Avenue, Macclesfield
1989	Rev. Stanley WEBB	The Manse, Gawsworth Road, Macclesfield
1991	Rev. Margaret LAWDAY	The Manse, Atholl Close, Macclesfield.
1996	Rev. Derrick BANNISTER	The Manse, Atholl Close, Macclesfield.

Aerial View of Langley 1999 ©

Chapel Interior 1953

Chapel Interior 1998

Flower Festival 1993

Flower Festival 1993

Annual Church Meeting 2003

Rev. Derrick Bannister and Church Officers 1998

9

Making Music

Music has always played an important role in the Methodist Church. Charles Wesley and other Methodists wrote many fine hymns that are sung today with the same enthusiasm as they were two hundred and fifty years ago.

Although very little is known about the design and structure of the first Chapel in Langley (1826 – 1856), we are informed that there was a Singing Loft for the Choir and that the choristers were accompanied by a clarinet and a horn.

When Sgt. Wardle's return from the Crimean War was celebrated in Langley during 1855, the singing was led by the Chapel Choir, in which the vocalists were: Mr Haytor, Mr Hesford, Mr Holland and Mr Moss. These singers were accompanied by the pianist Mr G Gee.

The present building, when opened as the second Chapel in 1858, had a Gallery or "Choir Loft". The Choir was accompanied by a clarinet (played by John Davies), a horn (played by Mr Ambrose) and a double-bass (played by Mr Hunt). On special occasions the music was supplemented by an orchestra of violins. In the 1860s a harmonium was introduced; initially this was played by Joseph Hunt and in later times the instrument was also played by Isaac Hesford and Mrs Mary Alice Moore.

Between 1860 and 1880 the Choirs of Langley Chapel and St. James' Church, Sutton, would visit each other's Church and sing together at special ecumenical services for Easter and Harvest Festivals.

After twenty years of using the Singing Loft, the Choir moved to its present position, left of the rostrum and next to the harmonium.

In 1883 the Trustees approved a plan to acquire an organ for the Chapel. The £220 needed for the purchase of this first organ was raised by means of a Sale of Work and a Bazaar. These events were organised by Mrs Ann Prichard acting as the Treasurer of the Organ Fund. (A similar challenge and solution arose in the early 1990s in connection with the acquisition and installation of the electronic organ.)

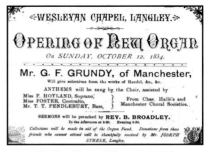

Dedication of Organ 1884

A dedication service for the new, small but well-built Stringer Pipe Organ was held on Sunday 12th October 1884. The Rev. B Broadly led this Service. Mr G Grundy, from Manchester, played the new organ, musical accompaniment was provided by instrumentalists of the well-known Hallé orchestra, and choral groups from Manchester sang songs of praise.

The Chapel Choir presented fund-raising concerts for the purchase of new music books and chant books for their own use.

In a letter written in her later years, Mrs Mary Alice Moore recalled that –

> *"a clock used to be positioned close to the Choir stalls. When it became clear that the Minister was delivering an over-long sermon, one of the members of the Choir would nudge the minute-hand forward by 15-minutes or so – when unobserved by the preacher."* Mrs Moore also reminisced about the 1880s when *"Thomas Wardle would attend services in Flash Chapel. After hearing new tunes there, he would sing them to me later and I would play the new music on the harmonium at the next Sunday service in Langley Chapel."*.

Mr Arthur Dale, the Choir Master, formed the Langley Choral Society. This Society gave it's first Concert on 18th January 1911, and then entered a number of competitions. In addition to the group winning prizes at the competitions, some of the members won individual awards.

Early members of the Choral Society included: Mrs R Massey; Mrs L Hammond; Mrs R Barton; Mr and Mrs Hartington Whiston, and Mr J Blackshaw.

Sometimes this Choral Society gave concerts to raise money for the Choir Fund, and on other occasions funds were raised for the Church's Overseas Missionary Work. The Society was disbanded at the end of 1919.

The Chapel Choir also presented fund-raising concerts. For instance at a concert in 1922 enough money was raised to purchase a piano, which they then presented to the Chapel. First to play the new piano was Miss Dorothy Warren. During the 1922 concert, songs were sung by Mrs Wilfred Massey, Miss Marion Heapy and Mr W Robinson.

Both the First World War and the Second World War had adverse effects on the Langley Chapel. During both conflicts many Langley residents served in the armed forces and one consequence was that the congregations were reduced, and so the Chapel Choirs were badly affected.

Langley Chapel Choir and Friends 1947

Shortly after WWII, in 1948, the Macclesfield Methodist Circuit organised the first annual Eisteddfod for all Methodist churches in the area, so they could work together again after the war years. The Langley Choir attained high standards at the first and second Eisteddfods. In 1950, and again in 1951, the Choir was awarded First Prize. (The last Macclesfield Eisteddfod was held in 1970.)

Rev. Margaret Lawday, Choir and Guest Preacher Rev. Margaret Cundiff c.1992

In the last half of the 20th century the Choir has sung regularly during Sunday Services in Langley Chapel and at many fund-raising functions. Also it has participated in exchange services with Sutton St. James' for Harvest Festivals and during Carol Services – emulating the special combined Services that took place during the decades between 1860 and 1880.

The accompanying photograph, taken in 1988, shows the Rev. Alan Ashley with some male members of the choir including: Rev. Tom Baird (Supernumerary Minister); Arthur Tatton (Local Preacher); Claude Harlington, MBE (Local Preacher); Philip Connor (organist); Roy Barber (choir member); Philip Wardle (organist), and Roger Preston (Local Preacher, organist and choir leader).

Rev. Alan Ashley and Choir Group c.1986

Regular performances have been presented by the choir since 1990 including fund-raising concerts for worth-while causes - such as the purchase of the electronic organ now in Langley.

Andrew Green Playing the New Organ at 1993 Flower Festival

The Stringer pipe organ was replaced after 108 years of regular use. In due course this 1884-vintage organ was moved to Rainow where it was added to the other venerable old pipe organs in the collection of Philip Torr. In 1991 an Organ Fund was formed and by 1992 it had raised £8,000 towards the purchase price of £16,000 for the present Makin Fanfare Digital Computer Organ.

Since 1996 a music group has augmented the organ music, especially during the monthly Family Service. In more recent times the group has added singing to the instruments that include piano, flute, recorder, guitar and bass guitar.

During the life of the Chapel various hymn books have been in regular use, including –

The Methodist Hymn Book, 1904– 1933;
The Methodist Hymn Book, 1933 – 1986;
Supplement Hymns and Songs, 1969 – 1986;
Hymns and Psalms, from 1986, and
Songs of Fellowship, from 1995.

At the Chapel Anniversary Concert held on 9th May 1998, the choir wore their new choir robes and sang a wide variety of music including hymns and excerpts from Gilbert and Sullivan, Flanders and Swan, and Scott Joplin. Soloists were Brenda Berry and Derek Lockett, while Kathryn Preston played the recorder. The pianists were Philip Wardle and Roger Preston.

Christmas-time carols are still sung door-to-door around the village. On two nights in December 2002 the sum of £297 was raised for the East Cheshire Hospice. On another night in the same week the augmented choir sang carols for the patients and staff in the Hospice.

<u>Organists and Choir Leaders.</u>

Organists	Choir Leaders
1858: Joseph HUNT	1858: Joseph HUNT
1880: Isaac HESFORD	1880: Fred MILLWARD
1880 – 1890: Mrs M A MOORE	from before 1911: Arthur DALE
1891 – 1916: Mr G WARDLE	
1916: James MAYCOCK	
1917: Miss L ANDERTON, & James MAYCOCK	
1920–1953: T Arthur WARDLE	1920: T Arthur WARDLE Leslie HAMMOND
1953 – 1958: Philip CONNOR	1953–1987: James BLACKSHAW
1958 – 1987: *rota* – Philip WARDLE, Harry WATERHOUSE, Philip CONNOR & Dora DEAN (*née* BARBER) (to 1960)	
1987 – 1996: *rota* Philip CONNOR (to 1994), Andrew GREEN (from 1992), Philip WARDLE, & Roger PRESTON	1987 – 1996: Katharine BARBER
1996 – 2002: *rota* – Roger PRESTON, & Philip WARDLE	1996 – 2002: Roger PRESTON
from 2002: *rota* – Philip WARDLE, Martin HEATHCOTE, & Pianist: John MOSS	from 2002: Derek LOCKETT

10

The Sunday School and Day School

<u>The Sunday School.</u>

When the first Wesleyan Chapel was built in 1826 weekly Sunday School classes were held in the premises. In those early days the Sunday School offered the only chance for many of the village children to receive formal religious instruction and to learn how to read and write.

In the 1860s Sunday School classes were held between Chapel Services. These were conducted by the Local Preachers who usually were assisted by wives, daughters and widows of the local manufacturers' families.

Mary Alice Moore,
John Thomas Moore and
Gertrude Moore c.1927

Some of the first Sunday School teachers were Mrs William Smith, Mrs Ann Prichard, Mr Hesford, Mr W I B Smith, Ralph Steele and Thomas Wardle. Most of these people continued teaching in the Sunday School until the 1880s.

Years later Mrs Mary Alice Moore recalled that the Sunday School in the second Chapel was held in the mornings between 9.30 and noon and between 1.30 p.m. and 2.30 p.m. after the Sunday Services. Reading and writing were taught during the morning sessions – for many children this was the only formal education that they were offered. Mrs Moore also wrote intriguingly about *"… teaching the children to make pot hooks."*. Thanks to Dennis Whomsley, in his book "Methodism in Macclesfield", those who are mystified can discover something about pot hooks! Mr Whomsley quotes Adam Rushton (1821 – 1909), a Macclesfield Methodist, who wrote about his experiences in the Sunday School at Hurdsfield where he learned how to write -

> *"In the Bible classes writing was taught. There I learned the joy of making straight strokes, pot hooks and ladles, and later came forth words and sentences, and even my own name written in large strokes of my quill pen."*.

Increased enrolments for the Sunday School led to the Long Room in the Wesleyan Chapel premises being altered in 1881. It was divided into two levels by the construction of a new floor, and it was subdivided permanently from the worship area by the construction of a solid wall – on which the "Ten Commandments" board was hung.

The Sunday School became increasingly successful: by 1892 it was attracting more than 140 scholars. At this time the School Supervisors were Ralph Steele and Thomas Wardle, the Treasurer was Joseph Steele, the Secretary was Mr J I Davidson and the Librarian was Herbert Warren. The Committee members were: Mrs Jane Smith, John Thomas Moore, Harold Whiston, Fred Millward, Miss Edith Whiston, Miss Marion Whiston, John Bailey, Miss Warren, John Shaw and Miss Louie Bay.

The need for more space, to accommodate the large number of children, was solved when the New Connexion Chapel (*"The Ebenezer"*) became vacant in 1892: it was rented for use as an overflow from the main Sunday School. The New Connexion Committee sold their prayer books and copy books to Harold Whiston for £13/-/-, for use by the children of the Langley Wesleyan Chapel Sunday School.

When the *"Ebenezer"* was brought into use during September 1892 there were two classes: in one were thirty children under the age of seven years, and in the other were thirty-two children aged fifteen and older. Children between these ages continued to attend the Sunday School in Langley Wesleyan Chapel.

Samuel Ball was appointed caretaker, to maintain the New Connexion property, at a wage of £1/5/- (*one pound and five shillings*) per year.

Two fund-raising Wesleyan Tea Meetings were held during 1892. One, on 22nd October, was for the Sunday School when Mr Potts played the violin, and duets were sung by Mr Wardle, Mrs Worth and Miss Millward. These performers were thanked formally by Mr F Milne. The second of these Meetings was held on 24th December when 240 adults and children sat down at 5.30 p.m. for the Tea. A Concert was presented by the children, accompanied by the children's choir: the leading performers were –

Harry Carlisle	*"Jack"*
Bertha Hammond	*"Jill"*
Jno Meakin	*"Jack Horner"*
Jas Hambleton	*"Boy Blue"*
May Dawson	*"Red Riding Hood"*
Muriel Whiston	*"Old Mother Hubbard"*
Miss G. Wardle	*"Mistress Mary"*

The Wesleyan Chapel premises were extended again in 1896 to accommodate the nearly 200 Sunday School children who were now in attendance. The two-storey addition to the Chapel, funded by William Whiston, included class rooms, a lavatory; and a vestry. At that time the Superintendent of the Sunday School was Miss Edith Whiston and the Treasurer was William Whiston.

Another extension was made to the Chapel premises in 1911 to further enlarge the space

Langley Sunday School Football Team 1923

available for the Sunday School. This addition was a gift from William Whiston.

The extra space enabled concerts and plays to be staged by the pupils. Not long after the 1911 extension was opened, as a commemoration for King George V's Coronation, *"Snow White"* was performed by the Sunday School.

Annual Summer outings and other events were organized for the Sunday School pupils. A highlight of these special occasions was the presentation of prizes, usually books and certificates, for regular attendance and good work. Outings were made to Southport, Rudyard Lake, Buxton and other nearby places of interest, where the children would play organised games after which they had a picnic and were usually given an orange as a gift.

The minute book records that in 1935 the outing was to Southport. Each adult had to pay 1/6 (*one shilling and six pence*) and the children were charged 9d (*nine pence*) each. These charges covered transport and a sandwich tea at *"Salt's Café"* at 5 p.m. Three children had to occupy two adult seats on the coach.

Miss Edith Whiston formed a Band of Hope with eight young members of the Sunday School in 1888, and by 1908 eighty-eight had enrolled. The support given to Miss Whiston encouraged her to establish a Temperance Society for adults which in 1908 had 54 members. Edith Whiston was assisted by her brother Harold and Fred Millward: both groups encouraged abstinence from alcohol. The Band and the Society disbanded before the end of the First World War.

<u>1929/30, and 1938.</u>

In 1929 and 1930 Anniversary Services and Tea Parties were organised. Each year there was also a Walk of Witness around the village, accompanied by the Langley Print Works Band.

Miss Louie Bay conducted a choir of 64 children in 1938 during the 80th Anniversary Service. After the Service the children attended Sunday School, and each was given an orange as a treat.

Walk of Witness c.1980

<u>Sunday School in the 'fifties, and later.</u>

Throughout the 1950s an enthusiastic group of workers devoted many hours of their time to the 60 children who attended the Sunday School.

Amongst these volunteers was Miss Dora Barber (now Mrs Philip Wardle) who was the morning Superintendent and Teacher; she was also Secretary of the Junior Missionary Association, and Leader of the Youth Club. Other hard-working volunteers included: Philip Wardle, Wilf Avery, John Manifold, Jean Bullock, Phyllis Barber and Betty Barton.

By 1962 the enrolment at the Sunday School had dropped to 34 children, probably because of the increasing variety of alternative "attractions" and changing social circumstances. Whatever the reasons, by the end of the 20th century enrolments for the Sunday School had declined further.

Until 1985 an annual event was the Sunday School Anniversary (the Sermons). A feature of these Anniversary events was the Walk of Witness around the village reminiscent of the 1929/30 era when the Langley Print Works Band accompanied the children during their Walks.

Sunday School Anniversary 1970

Cast of Sunday School Play 1972

Junior Church, and Sunday Club.

In 1986 the name of the Sunday School was changed to Junior Church, which later became the Sunday Club.

By 2000 attendance at the Sunday Club had dropped. It rarely exceeded six children, none over the age of eleven years.

Janette and Julian Cherryman at Anna's Baptism 2003

The recent Sunday School (Junior Church / Sunday Club) Superintendents were: May Wilson, 1966 – 1973; Alan Chapman, 1973 – 1985; Anne Preston, 1985 – 1991; Jane Fernyhough, 1991 – 1994; Jenny Lewis, 1994 - 2000; and Karen Horrocks, from 2000.

Cradle Roll.

Contact is maintained with the parents of children who have been baptised at Langley Chapel. Normally birthday cards are sent, together with invitations to special services such as *"Christingle"* at Christmas time.

Mothers' Committee.

In the 1970s a group of mothers in the village got together to encourage and support work in the Sunday School. Normally they met in the Langley Institute, now known as The Village Hall. This group arranged various activities including outings and a New Year's Concert (held in the Chapel premises) for children who attended a Sunday School – members of Sunday Schools outside Langley were welcomed.

The mothers also organised a Keep Fit Club for themselves, held during day-time hours in the Village Hall.

The Day School.

The success of the Sunday School led to the formation of the Wesleyan Day School within the Chapel premises during 1870. The first teacher was Mr Samuel Young. By 1875 Mr Young had more than 75 children attending his classes: this number of pupils was too great for the room available.

The Education Act of 1870 enabled the setting-up of locally-elected School Boards, and it made education compulsory for children between the ages of five and thirteen, although some children over the age of ten could be exempted. The Act also set standards for all Charity Schools.

William Whiston responded to the need for larger Day School premises by purchasing a piece of land in Main Road, Langley, for a new building. In 1877 the Langley Board School was built on the land. This was opened on 14th January 1878 by the Head Master Mr James Cotterell, accompanied by his wife Mrs Ellen Cotterell, in the presence of the Board Chairman, Mr William Whiston, and members of the Committee (including Mr W I B Smith and Mr Macey).

At the Opening were seventy-seven boys and girls, and four more scholars were

November 9th, 1895		
William BAND	Church View, Land Ends	Manufacturer
Walter BAILEY	Walker Lane	Silk dyer
Chas BAILEY		Silk Dyer
Ralph BULLOCK	Jarman Farm	Farmer
John SLATER	Sutton Hall Farm	Farmer
Joseph HIRST	Gurnett	Coalman
John DOWNES	Langley	Silk printer
Jas DAWSON	Langely	Print cutter
Thos MEAKIN	Langley	Silk dyer
Isaac HESFORD	Langley Hall	Farmer / butcher
Daniel BALL	Langley	Provision dealer
Samuel SIMPSON	Langley	Silk printer
Harry MILLWARD	Langley	Block cutter
Fred. DOWNES	Langley Hall Yard	Silk printer
Fred WARDLE	Langley Hall Yard	Silk printer
John DOWNES	Langley	Silk printer
William DOWNES	Langley	Silk printer
William HINE	Langley	Block cutter
Philip MILLWARD	Langley	Block printer
James RATHBONE	Sutton	Stone merchant
Herbert PHILIPS, JP	Sutton Oaks	-
Henry MALBON	Oak Grove	Steward
William ROBINSON	Ridge Hall Farm	Farmer
Thomas COOPER	Fox Bank	Farmer
Edith Lilian WHISTON	Clough House	Gentlewoman
John DAVIDSON	The Shubberies	Colour mixer
John WARREN	54 Langley	Pattern maker

Nominations for Langley Board School 1895

admitted to the school on the following day. Each scholar paid 4d (four-pence) each week for their education. The Government paid a small grant to cover the wages of the Head Master. Langley Chapel had to provide the furniture, books and slates and also had to meet the costs of heating and maintaining the School.

Reading, writing and arithmetic were taught by the Head Master. Subjects such as drawing, singing and sewing were taught by volunteers including Mrs Ann Prichard, Mrs Warrington, Miss Ball, Mrs William Smith and Mr Hesford.

An Assistant Mistress, Miss Perkins, was appointed in 1879 at an annual salary of £67.

Her Majesty's Inspector reported on 8th March 1879 that-

> " ... considering the short period the School has been open, the results are creditable to the master. ... 1st and 2nd Standards, _ of the students are good; Writing shows careful instruction; Geography (is) fair ...Average Pass (is) 90 per cent ... "

Boys who worked in the Print Works attended the school as "Half Timers": during one week they worked each morning and spent their afternoons as scholars, and the next week their mornings were spent at school and they reverted to being wage-earners in the afternoons. The Print Works owner, Mr Whiston, was very strict; on one occasion he sent the following note to the Head of the School -

> "I observed eight boys loitering on the road at 9.25 a.m. They are to be told that they will not be admitted late and consequently will lose half a day's work worth six-pence, as they may not work until they make up school time.".

In 1882 Mr William Parkinson became the new Head Master. His first entry in the school's Log Book reads –

> "Took charge of this school, found children disposed to test the strength of their new master. Some difficulty in writing because there are no pens and no ink.".

Langley Board School 1907
Headmaster Mr J J Cragg & Teacher Miss Louie Bay

The quotations above from Mr Whiston and Mr Parkinson indicate that life in Langley during the late 19th century had some similarities with life in the early 21st century!

School Inspectors examined the children in reading and writing every year.

Langley Methodists relinquished control of the Board School after The Education Act of 1902 abolished School Boards and transferred their functions to County Councils. The Macclesfield Education Committee became responsible for managing the Board Schools in the local area.

Mr Willdig became Headmaster in 1898 and stayed until 1906. Mr Willdig was followed by Mr John J Cragg of Rainow; Miss Louie Bay became his assistant teacher.

Mr Cragg remained in the post until his death in 1937; he was succeeded by Mrs Slaney. Mrs Slaney was appointed Headmistress at a time when 59 children were enrolled in the school.

Mrs Ashness took over from Mrs Slaney in 1951 and remained Headmistress until the school was closed. Due to an exceptionally large intake of children to the Day School in 1967 more classroom space was required. After lengthy negotiations between the Trustees of Langley Chapel and the Education Department it was agreed that the School would rent the Sunday School room, cloakroom, toilets and parking area – to be used as the playground – for the sum of £280 per year. This arrangement remained in place until 26th March 1970, when the children from Langley (Board) School and the children of St. James' Church of England School were moved into the newly constructed Hollinhey County Primary School at Sutton Lane Ends.

In October 1970 the former Langley school building was opened as a Teachers Centre and remained in use until 2002, when it was sold and became a private house.

Langley Board School c.1980

11

Langley Hall Estate

The first mention of Langley Hall and its Estate of about 220 acres was in 1651 when William Clowes (16?? – 1693), of *"Whiteleigh"* in the Cheshire village of Wincle, married Katherine (1621 – 1693), a daughter and heiress of Robert Yeveley, of Langley Hall.

Robert Yeveley died in 1671 and the Langley Hall Estate then passed into the ownership of the Clowes family.

It is not known when the Hall was built, or who built it, but clearly stone from the Tegg's Nose quarry was used extensively for constructing the walls. It is known that the beautiful Queen Anne canopy over the main door was erected in 1696 by William and Mary Clowes who were residing in the Hall at that time.

Charles Clowes (1747 – 1818), a manufacturer and cotton bleacher, built the *"Bollinhead Mill"* and a number of cottages on the Estate before 1790. From this date the hamlet of Langley grew more rapidly, within the boundary of the Estate.

Important supplies of clear water pass through the Estate. Two streams, one being the River Bollin, join close to Langley Hall. A third stream, which rises above *"Pyegreave Farm"*, also joins the River Bollin near the Hall: although this supplies only a relatively

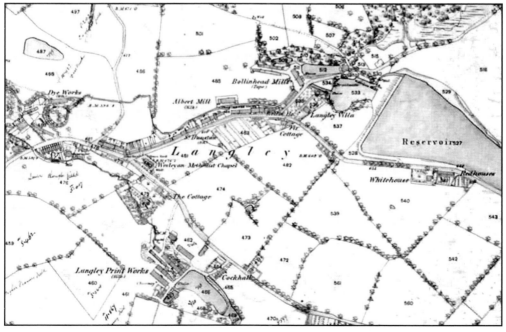

Langley Map c.1871

low daily volume, its water is exceptionally pure. The combination of quantity, falls and quality of the different streams in Langley has attracted a number of textile manufacturers, including silk printers, over the decades.

The Estate was sold in 1806 to David Yates (1733 – 1812), of Manchester, when he was a 73-year-old cotton bleacher and silk manufacturer. This David Yates proceeded to build cottages in Langley: he leased some of the property and some land to other manufacturers involved with textiles. His son, David Yates (1761 – 1827), inherited the Estate in 1812 and continued to develop the hamlet by building additional terraced cottages and the *"St. Dunstan"* public house, and also by contributing to the building of the first Wesleyan Chapel, which was opened in 1826. David Yates "II" was the last resident-owner of the Hall.

After the death of David Yates *"II"* the Langley Hall Estate was put up for sale in 1828. Information in a sale advertisement placed in the *"Macclesfield Courier"* indicates what Estate properties were included, where people were living and, in some cases, what their occupations were at that time-

> *The three mills known as the* "Bollinhead Mills" *were being leased to Isaac Smith, the smallwares manufacturer.*
>
> *The Print Works in Cockhall Lane (consisting of a mill, a dye house, a warehouse and five stone cottages) were leased to William Smith, the silk printer.*
>
> *Henry Yates had built a house in Main Road called* "The Firs".
>
> *Six stone cottages stood between Langley Hall and the River Bollin. One was empty and the others were being rented to: James Warren, Henry Bradley, Josiah Lomas, John Hudson, and John Smith a nephew of Isaac Smith.*
>
> *The newly-built* "St. Dunstan" *public house, complete with a brew-house, stables and slaughter-house, was leased to Ralph Birchenall.*
>
> *Six brick cottages attached to the public house were occupied by: Isaac Gee, Joseph Day, John Yates, John Grimshaw, John Harrison, and Sam Poser.*
>
> *Another two cottages adjoining the public house were being leased to William Ratcliffe, and Joseph Warren.*
>
> *William Morley, another nephew of Isaac Smith's, had moved into premises now known as "15 Main Road". These premises included a shop, a bake house, a barn, shippons and a farmhouse that had been built around 1740.*

In 1831 Isaac Smith arranged a bank loan so that he could buy the Langley Hall Estate from the Yates family. Isaac Smith subdivided the Hall, and separate residences were then rented to tenants who worked on farms and in Langley mills.

Although Isaac Smith's smallwares business did not grow significantly in Langley, he continued the practice of renting land and buildings to other manufacturers: Isaac Smith's principal tenant was William Smith (no relation) who was expanding his Silk Print Works on the Cockhall Lane site in Langley.

In 1850 a small area of the Langley Hall Estate, and also some adjoining land owned by Lord Bingham, were acquired by the Macclesfield Corporation for the creation of two reservoirs, *"Ridgegate"* and *"Bottoms"*. A third reservoir, *"Teggsnose"*, was built during 1871 entirely on Lord Bingham's land.

These reservoirs were required to provide "compensation water" for the increasing number of water-powered mills in Macclesfield: the natural fluctuating flow along the River Bollin caused problems for the mill owners. The reservoirs also offered a solution to the problem of the river becoming ever more polluted with industrial and domestic wastes, especially in drought conditions. To serve their purposes the reservoirs had to discharge a total of 520,00 gallons a day into the River Bollin.

Within the Langley Hall Estate by 1870 there were about 130 dwellings, the *"Bollinhead Mills"*, the *"Albert Mill"*, the *"Dye Works"*, *"Langley Mill"*, the *"Print Works"*, some storage buildings, two farms, a slaughter house, a public house, some shops, at least one smithy, a shoe maker and clog repairer, the New Connexion Chapel, and Langley Wesleyan Chapel.

Albert Mill and Mr W Band 1890

William Whiston, who had inherited the Print Works from his uncle John Smith, developed the business until in 1892 it had become one of the largest hand-block silk printers in the British Isles – and it was exporting much of its product. By this stage in his life William Whiston could afford to purchase the Langley Hall Estate for £12,000, and in 1894 he paid £48,000 to Lord Lucan for the 1,200 acre Sutton Hall Estate.

The First World War brought many changes to the village. Almost one hundred men who worked in the hand block silk printing business now known as *"William Whiston and Son"* joined the army or navy. The loss of their skills and the decline in demand for luxury printed silks combined to affect the business quite badly. The effect was made worse when William Whiston died in May 1915, the year after WWI had started. William Whiston's death at the age of 77 was not only a loss to his family but to the village as well. Over many years he had been a dominant leader and innovator in both his business and Langley life, and he had invested wisely in the silk printing enterprise and in numerous local community projects.

After World War I the profitability of a number of businesses in Britain, including some textile companies, declined: in 1929 some of these textile companies including, Whiston's of Langley and Brocklehurst's of Macclesfield, were joined together to form *"Brocklehurst Whiston Amalgamated Ltd."* (BWA). Although part of BWA continued with silk-printing in Langley, on sites that had once been part of the Estate, the villagers had already begun to take more control over their own destinies and were relying less on the local Print Works and its owners.

The introduction of frequent bus services between Langley and Macclesfield enabled Langley residents to obtain employment outside the village.

Following the transfer of ownership of William Whiston and Son to BWA, village residents were offered the opportunity to purchase the cottages which they were renting and occupying. Many tenants took-up this offer.

It was in 1942 that the Langley Hall Estate became Freehold. The Second World War delayed the Commissioner of Crown Lands from issuing the Certificates of Freehold until September 1950. In a letter to the Chapel Trustees about the finalisation of this matter, Harold Whiston wrote *"It has been a long and tedious job and the money it cost to do it has been preposterous"*.

By the early 1960s the *"Bollinhead Mills"* and the *"Albert Mill"* had been demolished: houses now stand on both sites.

In 1984 Langley Hall and the adjoining buildings were sold to Willan Homes. This developer then carefully renovated the property, making three large apartments within the Hall and nine mews cottages in the area where farm buildings had stood.

BWA closed its works in Cockhall Lane, Langley during 1964, and the Print Works site was sold to *"Ernest Scragg and Son"*, manufacturers of textile machinery. In 1986 ownership of the site changed to the Swiss firm *"Reiter-Scragg"*, who continued to manufacture textile machinery in Langley until 2000. In the Millennium year Reiter-Scragg transferred their operation, and workforce, from the village to a factory in Lyme Green, near Macclesfield. The Cockhall Lane site in Langley is awaiting new owners, and redevelopment [*early 2003*].

All the children of William and Emma Whiston had died by 1971, and their descendants had moved away from Langley. After almost two centuries the last link between the Estate and the two pioneering Smith families was broken early in 2003 when a field near the site of the original Dye Works was sold. The vendor was descended from both Isaac Smith, who once owned the Estate, and William Smith, who first used indigo dye to print silk in buildings on the Estate rented from Isaac Smith.

Two of the original mill-sites in Langley still being used for commercial purposes [*early 2003*], in modernised buildings, are –

The old *"Langley Mill"*, in Langley Road, is occupied by *"Specialised Automobile Services"*, makers of rims and wheel centres for vehicles dating from Victorian times to the present day.

What was the *"Dye Works"*, close to Langley Hall, now houses the *"Adamley / David Evans"* division of Silk Industries PLC. This firm screen-prints silks for another specialist market.

It is possible that the earliest silk-printing by William Smith, using indigo and other natural dyes, was undertaken on or close to the same Dye Works site that

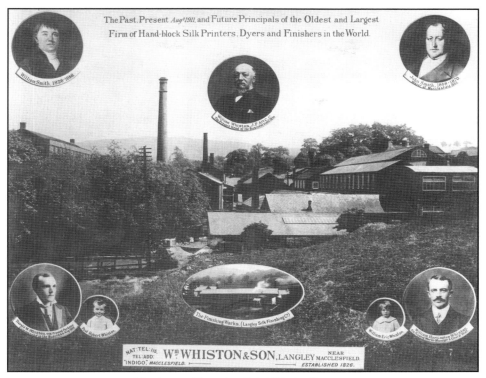

Montage of Langley Print Works Owners
1820 - 1911

Adamley / David Evans is now using for their *"high tech"* procedures. The same source of particularly pure water that the pioneering hand-block silk printer relied on is still needed by the modern silk screen printer. The uncommon qualities of this water are enabling the tradition of producing prestigious printed silk to continue on what was the Langley Hall Estate.

12

Langley Notables

The Isaac Smith and the William Smith family trees.

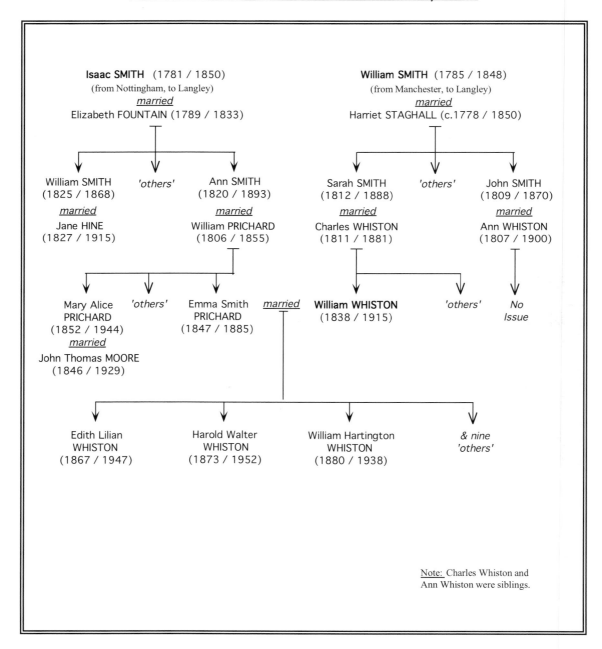

Note: Charles Whiston and
Ann Whiston were siblings.

Isaac Smith: 1781 – 1850.

Isaac Smith was a cotton bleacher and smallwares manufacturer. After moving from Nottingham, Isaac Smith started his business in Langley during 1815. He had moved north with his wife Elizabeth (*née* Fountain) and his nephews John Smith and William Morley. (Elizabeth's mother, Mrs Elizabeth Fountain, probably moved to Langley at some stage: a plaque in the Langley Chapel is to an 'Elizabeth Fountain' who was not Isaac Smith's wife.)

Isaac Smith 1781 - 1850

Isaac Smith rented a cottage and the *"Bollinhead Mill"* from David Yates, the owner of the Langley Hall Estate. The residence, *"Holehouse Cottage"*, was in what was then called *"Bollin Lane"* and is now *"Holehouse Lane"*. The cottage has been sub-divided into *"Rock Cottage"* and *"Rose Cottage"*. The mill, which was approached from the lane, has been dismantled.

During his first few years in Langley, Isaac Smith conducted his smallwares manufacturing business with some commercial success. In 1831 he was able to purchase the 220-acre Langley Hall Estate, which included a number of mill buildings, from the Yates family. To make the purchase, Isaac Smith took a loan of £12,000 with the Brocklehurst Bank of Macclesfield.

Holehouse Cottage
1890

Around 1828 Isaac Smith built *"Bollin House"* to accommodate himself, his wife and their seven children. Isaac's wife Elizabeth and their sons Isaac and John died before 1836.

Although Isaac Smith was an Anglican, he became involved with the Langley Methodists, and he provided significant financial support for the construction of their first Chapel. In 1838 he made a gift to twelve Trustees of the Title of the land on which the Chapel and graveyard had been developed. The Macclesfield Methodist Preachers Meeting records that Isaac Smith had become a local preacher sometime before 1839.

Isaac Smith died of cholera in 1850. Although he had paid interest regularly on the £12,000 loan, borrowed in 1831, he had repaid none of the principal and so, as a consequence, his Will was held in Chancery until 1892 when William Whiston – now the wealthy owner of the Print Works – settled the debt with Brocklehurst Bank.

William Smith (1825 – 1868), a son of Isaac and Elizabeth, and his sister Ann (1820 – 1893), grew-up to become very active Langley Methodists. (William married Jane Hine from the Buxton area, and Ann married William Prichard who moved to Langley from Manchester and had interests in smallwares manufacturing.)

In Langley Chapel there is a marble memorial to Isaac Smith and his family. A separate tablet is to an Elizabeth Fountain who was probably Isaac's mother-in-law. Also one of the stained glass windows is in the name of William Smith (1825 – 1868), one of the sons of Isaac and Elizabeth.

The Prichard Family:

William Prichard married Ann Smith, a daughter of Isaac & Elizabeth Smith, in 1844. William and Ann Prichard had two daughters (Emma and Mary Alice) who carried on their family's traditional support of Methodism – *see the family trees.*

Ann Prichard
1820 - 1893

Mrs Ann Prichard taught in both the Sunday School and the Day School; she also acted as Class Leader for the Chapel. In 1868 Mrs Prichard became the Chapel's Treasurer – she kept a firm hand on the purse strings, and never allowed the Chapel to go into debt. The Methodist account books record that while Mrs Prichard was Treasurer the Chapel's funds were healthier than the funds for any other Chapel in the Macclesfield Circuit.

William and Ann Prichard lived in *"Woodvilla"*, Langley. As a widow, Ann opened her house to all Methodists Preachers during their visits to the village. When Ann Prichard's grandson enquired, in 1888, where he might find the Rev. Woodward Spencer Mrs Prichard's answer was *"He's in the garden burning his Idol"* – smoking inside *"Woodvilla"* either was prohibited totally or Rev. Spencer burned a particularly pungent tobacco in his pipe! *"Woodvilla"* is now called *"Cherrywood"*.

Mrs Ann Prichard died peacefully during January 1893, just after she had walked home following a Sunday Service. She had devoted much of her life to Methodism (including the Chapel and the Sunday School), and her death was a great loss to the village.

One of the four stained glass memorial windows in Langley Chapel commemorates the life of Mrs Ann Prichard.

The Moore family:

One of the grand-daughters of Isaac and Elizabeth Smith was Mary Alice Prichard (1852 – 1944) who was born in Langley. She married John Thomas Moore (1846 – 1929) in 1872 at the Brunswick Chapel in Macclesfield. They had six children, three of whom survived infancy.

Following their marriage Mr & Mrs Moore lived in Macclesfield before moving to Crewe. They had shops in both towns, including a drapery business.

In 1887 the Moore family settled in *"Woodvilla"*, Langley. John Thomas Moore ("JTM") manufactured his patented folding chairs and tables in the *"Bollinhead Mill"*, Langley. He and his wife were deeply religious. They carried on the Prichard tradition of hosting Methodist Preachers when they were on visits to Langley Chapel.

For more than 30 years JTM taught in the Sunday School, and Mary Alice was a Sunday School teacher for 40 years. As the Circuit Magazine Secretary for Langley she delivered magazines to homes and farms, in all weathers.

As well as being an excellent pianist Mary Alice accompanied the Choir on the harmonium and later on the organ. She loved the Chapel and all it stood for: her faith was blended with kindness and good deeds.

J.T. and M.A. Moore had two daughters: Evelyn Prichard Moore (who qualified as a musician, and married the educationalist Professor Frank Smith, of Macclesfield), and Gertrude Alice Moore (who remained a spinster but devoted her life to the Langley Methodist Chapel).

A plaque in Langley Chapel is to members of the Moore family: John Thomas Moore, Mary Alice Moore and Gertrude Alice Moore.

Miss Gertrude Alice Moore: (1874 – 1954)

In 1892 Miss Gertrude Moore became a Sunday School teacher in Langley and she taught in that capacity for 54 years. She was: a Trustee for the Chapel; an accredited Local Preacher; President of the Langley Methodist Women's Meeting, and a devoted worker for the Overseas Missions.

William Smith: 1786 – 1848, and his family.

In 1819 William Smith moved from Manchester to Langley. (No trace of the ancestry of this William Smith has been discovered.) The important, known fact is that he rented a building, close to Langley Hall and situated on a bank of the fast flowing Bollin River, from David Yates.

William Smith 1786 –1848
Founder of the Print Works

William Smith converted the building into a mill in which he started-up a business for dying and hand-printing silk fabric with indigo, using a wax-resist technique. Later he experimented with other coloured dyes which he extracted from local plants. His business grew until the small, rented mill became inadequate for his needs so, in 1826, he began building the Langley Print Works on land rented from David Yates, just off Cockhall Lane – which was once called *"Dirty Lane"*.

William Smith and his family lived in Langley Hall until around 1825 when they then moved to a cottage in Cockhall Lane (or *"Dirty Lane"*), near to the Print Works.

The family were Anglicans and they supported St. James' Church, Sutton with many financial donations.

William and Harriet spent the last years of their lives in *"Rock House"*, which they built in 1843 on the corner of Bullocks Lane and Byrons Lane, Sutton.

When he died in 1848, aged 63, William Smith left £180 to St. James' Church.

In St. James' Church is a memorial to William and Harriet Smith. The Millennium Plaque in Langley commemorates William Smith and his pioneering silk printing enterprise.

The silk-printing business prospered and after his death the business passed into the ownership of William's son John Smith.

John Smith: 1808 – 1870.

John Smith
1808 - 1870

Like his father, John was an Anglican. During the era of his ownership, the Langley Print Works continued to develop. John Smith, who had married Ann Whiston in 1829, built his family's residence *"The Cottage"* in Dirty Lane (later renamed *"Clough House"* in *"Cockhall Lane"*) in 1834. Whatever John's personal contributions might have been to the Works, he had a number of interests outside his Langley business: he was a leading Freemason in an area that embraced Stockport, Congleton and Macclesfield, and his involvement in civic affairs led to him serving as the Mayor of Macclesfield during 1853/54 – when he fired a ceremonial cannon in West Park to announce the fall of Sebastopol in the Crimea. John Smith also involved himself in the affairs of both Langley Chapel, to which he gave financial support, and St. James' Church, Sutton.

John Smith helped with the planning and design of St. James' Church, in 1839, and he was one of the first five Trustees and also the Chairman of the Building Committee. He and his wife attended St. James' regularly, using their family pew, and in 1861 John Smith served as a church warden at St. James'. After his death, his Masonic brethren erected a large memorial window to him in the chancel behind the altar at St. James' Church.

John Smith's interests and contributions were not confined to the Anglicans' St. James': during 1857/58 he was involved with the planning and design of Langley Chapel and also he gave generous financial gifts to the building fund.

John Smith and his wife Ann remained childless. However John trained his young and, apparently, very able nephew William Whiston to run the Print Works. During the last years of his life John became freer to devote his energies to his Civic and Masonic interests because he could rely on his nephew to manage the printing business. When he died in 1870, William Whiston became the owner of the silk-printing concern.

William Whiston: 1838 – 1915.

William Whiston was the son of Charles and Sarah Whiston. Charles (1811 – 1881) had been born at *"Pyegreave Farm"*, Langley. Sarah (1812 – 1888) was a daughter of William and Harriet Smith, and a sister of John, who owned the Print Works.

Young William Whiston spent more time with his childless uncle and aunt, John and Ann Smith of Langley, than with his parents, Charles and Sarah Whiston – who spent their working lives in Macclesfield and Sutton. Mrs John Smith was a sister of Charles Whiston - *see the family trees*.

William Whiston inherited the Langley Print Works business in 1870; it then became *"William Whiston"* and in 1896 its name was changed to *"William Whiston and Son"*. While under William Whiston's control, the hand-block silk-printing enterprise expanded.

From 1870 additional buildings were erected on the Cockhall Lane site and the business eventually used all other mill buildings in Langley. Between 1894 and 1911 Whiston's of Langley bought-out nearly every other silk-printing business in England, and for a few years they exported Langley prints to America, Africa, Rangoon and India. Their work-force increased significantly between 1870 and the First World War, when additional workers walked daily between Macclesfield and the Print Works. Many of these commuters wore clogs – which made a unique noise on hard surfaces; the shoe-maker in Langley also made and repaired clogs.

Whiston's business grew largely because of the dedication and skills of the local craftspeople. Villagers were trained, and encouraged to perfect their skills, in the arts of design, dye-making, colour-matching, block-making, printing and in all the other essential tasks.

Most of the people employed in the Print Works lived in Langley – where many of the cottages had been built for Smith businesses and were now owned by William Whiston. The Print Works was involved actively in sundry aspects of the villagers' social lives and it

William Whiston and Family
at Clough House 1894

helped to provide various amenities including the Institute, the cricket field, a pension scheme and the Board School. The Print Works and Langley Chapel were interlinked closely both inside and outside each organisation. For example, learning and self-development for commercial and broader reasons were mutually beneficial and seemed to be in harmony with ideas that John Wesley had preached.

The telegraphic address for the "William Whiston" Print Works was *'Indigo Langley'*.

In 1865 William Whiston married Emma Smith Prichard, a grand-daughter of Isaac and Elizabeth Smith. (Emma's mother, Ann was a Sunday School teacher in Langley before she married William Prichard in 1844.) Unlike her husband, Emma was a Methodist. With William she had twelve children; nine survived beyond infancy, and a number became active Methodists in Langley. Their sons Harold and Hartington joined their father in his Langley silk-printing business.

William and Emma, and their children, probably regarded *"Clough House"*, Cockhall Lane, Langley, as their real family home. Some members of the family continued to live in it until 1957.

Clearly Emma influenced her husband to assist the Langley Methodists in a variety of ways. In 1891 William Whiston became the Treasurer for the Chapel, and continued in this capacity until his death in 1915. Tradition suggests that on Sundays William Whiston often looked-out from *"Clough House"* noting who entered the Chapel; any of his employees who missed a Service were, apparently, asked for their "excuse" when back at work on the following Monday. If true, then it is an example of an Anglican helping Methodists in a particular manner because poor excuses were not tolerated!

Hartington and Marjorie Whiston c.1910

Emma died in 1885 when aged just 37-years. William's second wife, Louisa, looked after Emma's children who adored her. Included amongst the nine youngsters were Edith Lilian, Harold Walter and William Hartington.

One of the stained glass windows in the Chapel is to the memory of William Whiston, and another commemorates Emma's short life.

William Whiston never became a Methodist, but remained an Anglican. Over the years William Whiston kept a family pew in St. James' Church, Sutton and he supported that Church financially. Also he served there as a Church Warden in 1866, 1867 and 1874, and then became a Senior Trustee. At the end of the 19th C William Whiston paid for a new bell in St. Michael's Parish Church, Macclesfield.

William Whiston acquired ownership of the Langley Hall Estate in 1894 and in 1896 he purchased the Sutton Hall Estate – apparently in the expectation that his family would be pleased to move into more spacious accommodation, but his unmarried daughters elected to remain in Langley and so they continued to live in *"Clough House"*, with

Edith Whiston c.1910

their step-mother Louisa and their father – who died in *"Clough House"* in 1915.

Miss Edith L. Whiston: 1867 – 1947.

Edith never married and lived all her life in Langley where she devoted much of her energy to the Methodists' cause. For some years "Miss Edith" ran the Sunday School when more than 150 children attended..

Edith used to cycle around Langley and district visiting sick people, collecting rents and providing food when families were in need.

The playing field, on which many of the village's fetes and games are now held, was gifted to Langley *"… for all time …"* by Miss Edith Whiston.

After the death of William, her father, Edith Whiston became the owner of *"The St. Dunstan"* public house. How she coped with that responsibility when she was also active with The Temperance Society (which had a peak membership in Langley of 70), and with the Band of Hope, has not been recorded. Whatever conflicts she might have faced, Miss Edith Whiston collected the rent for many years from the landlords of the *"St Dunstan".*

One of the plaques in Langley Chapel is in memory of Edith Whiston.

Harold Walter Whiston: 1873 – 1952, and his wife Alice.

"HWW" was a son of William and Emma. In his own manner, Harold Whiston was an active Methodist. He understudied his father at the Langley Print Works until he became the *"governing director"* after William Whiston died in 1915.

At various times, Harold Whiston held almost every office at the Langley Chapel, including Deputy Superintendent of the Sunday School and Circuit Steward. Harold Whiston was a Local Preacher and often delivered lengthy sermons to Chapel congregations in Langley and Macclesfield.

Marriage of Harold Whiston and Alice Proctor 1896

HWW introduced a number of newly developed technologies to the Print Works including electricity, typewriters and telephone. He was aware that the company should not continue to be totally reliant on hand-block silk printing and so screen printing was introduced. Harold Whiston flew frequently on business around Europe in Imperial Airways' aircraft.

While Harold Whiston had a major control over it, the Print Works acquired a fire engine, which was made available for needs in the village, captained and crewed by Works' employees. Also a Print Works band was created. After WWII Harold Whiston started to sell some of the tythed cottages to the families living in them.

Harold Whiston's life is commemorated in Langley Chapel with a plaque.

In 1929 "William Whiston & Son" merged with "J T Brocklehurst & Son" to form *"Brocklehurst Whiston Amalgamated Ltd."* (BWA). Silk printing continued in Langley until 1964 when many thousands of the unique wooden printing blocks were scrapped, although a number were transferred to Italy for safe-keeping. The Silk Museum, Macclesfield, is now in possession of a collection of the pattern books, some sample blocks and various other items from the once-great silk-printing enterprise in Langley.

Harold Whiston married Alice Proctor of Macclesfield in 1896. As Mrs Harold Whiston she paid for the first electric lighting installation in Langley Chapel.

Miss Louie Bay: 1883 - 1939.

Miss Louie Bay was born in Langley in 1883. She grew-up in a loving Methodist family. Her father was employed as a designer in the Langley Print Works.

Miss Bay was a teacher in the Langley Board School and in the Sunday School. Louie Bay also trained many children to sing in Services held at the Chapel. She was much respected and loved by her numerous pupils and by her fellow teachers.

In an appreciation for her life, Mr C H Dawson wrote that Miss Bay was –

Louie Bay c.1930

> *"... a very much respected school teacher both in the day school and the Sunday School, a great worker among children ..."*

A memorial tablet to Miss Louie Bay is in Langley Chapel.

The Steele family:

Ralph Steele (1808 – 1892) was for more than 50 years the Sunday School Superintendent, and Teacher. Ralph Steele worked for 70 years at the Langley Print Works.

Joseph Steele (1852 - 1927) a son of Ralph Steele, joined the Print Works as a Tierier, an assistant to the hand block printer and responsible for mixing the dyes, at the age of eight years old. He stayed with the firm for the next 60 years, the last 30 as Works Manager.

Joseph Steele was a member of the Methodist Chapel throughout his life; he served as a Trustee and also as Chapel Steward. For many years he was the Superintendent of the Sunday School, working closely with Miss Edith Whiston.

In 1872 Joseph Steele married William Whiston's cousin Harriet Smith (1850 – 1921). Mr & Mrs Joseph Steele lived at *"Mount Pleasant"* in Cockhall Lane (now demolished) between 1881 and 1921.

Arthur Pickford: 1891 – 1985.

Arthur Pickford was born in Langley in 1891, and from the age of five until his death he resided in *"Fold Cottage"*, Cockhall Lane. He attended the Langley Board School until he reached the age of twelve, then he became an apprentice block-cutter at the Print Works; where he practised the art of making printing blocks until he retired at the age of 70-years.

In 1921 Arthur married Florence Alice Legge; they had three children Mary, Robert and Margaret. Mrs Pickford died in 1952.

During World War II he was an air raid (ARP) warden, and also was the Chairman of The (forces') Comforts Fund.

Over the decades Arthur held many positions in the Print Works, in the village and in Langley Chapel. At work he represented his workmates in union affairs and was on the Print Works' sick club committee. He was a Parish Councillor for many years.

A staunch Methodist from his youth, Arthur held nearly every office in the Methodist Chapel, and in the Sunday School, Langley. As the Secretary for the Sunday School Arthur organised summer outings and the annual prize-giving ceremonies for the children. Also he served as a Governor of the Langley Board School. Arthur was the Secretary to the Chapel Trust, and also acted as a Poor Steward – in this office he had to collect pew rents from outlying farms and elsewhere.

For a while he was President of the Langley Burial Society, which operated between 1838 and 1971, when many of it's members and officials were Langley Methodists.

It was Arthur Pickford's idea to establish a Remembrance Fund: he was the Fund Treasurer from it's inception in 1950 until 1985.

Arthur Pickford loved and grew flowers. He was a founder, show exhibitor, committee member and life member of the Macclesfield District Chrysanthemum Society, and the National Society awarded a medal to him for his services.

In May 1985 his Chapel friends organised a Thanksgiving Party to *"… acknowledge the dedicated and faithful service he has given to our Chapel for so many years."*

In November 1985, aged 94 years, Arthur Pickford died. A wall plaque and a wooden cross have been placed in Langley Chapel as reminders of his life.

Arthur Pickford's daughter, Mrs Mary Ashton, a life-long Methodist and member of the choir, took over the role of Treasurer of the Remembrance Fund. It was Mrs Ashton's idea to start the Wednesday "coffee and chat" mornings in the Chapel premises following the closure of the village shop.

George Percival Naden: 1910 - 1994.

George Percival *"Percy"* Naden was born on 29th March 1910. He was a son of Thomas Percival Naden (1880 – 1946), who was a lifelong member of the Methodist Church.

Arthur Pickford and Percy Naden
1985

Along with his brother Winston and his older sister Phyllis, Percy grew up at the family farm *"Lake House Farm"*, Sutton. Percy attended Sutton School until aged 14 years when he left to help his father run Lake House Farm.

After the death of Thomas, Percy took over management of the farm, and from his father he also took over the Hollin Lane Chapel Sunday School. He ran this virtually single-handed, holding all the Chapel offices, until the late 1960s. Local people still recall Percy running the Hollin Lane Sunday School. Percy Naden attended Langley Chapel for the Evening Service.

When Hollin Lane was closed Percy and his wife Ruth, who he had married in 1956, transferred all their activities to Langley Chapel. In the late 1960s Percy took on the role of Treasurer at Langley from Walter Bloor, and he also joined Arthur Pickford as a Church Steward. Percy served as Treasurer until 1992 and he had to guide the finances through some difficult times, including severe dry rot in the worship area. As a Steward, Percy welcomed visiting preachers and put them at ease after he had ensured that all preparations for the service were in hand. The preachers often commented that they appreciated Percy's friendly assistance and helpful prayers.

Percy was a member of the Property Committee, and in 1992 he helped to remove the old "Stringer" pipe organ and the carpet from the Chapel. Percy was very happy in the company of others and enjoyed entertaining: at Christmas the carol singers were always pleased to be welcomed by him, especially after carolling in the cold around Langley.

Before WWII Percy was involved with the Langley and District Agricultural Show. During the War he was often on Fire Watching duty at Cleulow Cross.

For recreation, he was passionate about crown green bowling: for twenty years he was active in a number of capacities with the NFU Macclesfield Branch Bowling Club. Among his trophies he won the R A Stannier cup in 1984.

In the mid-1980s Percy and Ruth left the farm and moved to Walker Lane.

Cyril H. Dawson: 1906 – 1999.

Cyril was born in Langley, and educated firstly at the Langley Board School and then at the Macclesfield Grammar School. After leaving school, Cyril followed the footsteps of his grandfather and his father into the Langley Print Works, where he became a block designer and block cutter. When technology changed he became skilled with providing the needs of the firm's screen printers.

Cyril Dawson
1996

Both Cyril Dawson and his wife Elsie were Methodists who devoted much of their lives to Langley Chapel.

Cyril's earlier years covered the time when the Print Works and Methodism were closely involved with each other in Langley: he was one of the active links between these two entities. After 1964 when BWA closed-down in Langley, he helped to link the Chapel with the community.

For the Chapel, Cyril Dawson became a Trustee, a Chapel Steward and the Chapel Keeper, and he also dedicated time to the Sunday School.

Cyril was an energetic and experienced walker but he was not a car driver. However he travelled widely, locally and around other rural areas in Britain, usually with his camera. He was interested in both flora and fauna, especially birds, and he often visited sites around the north coast of Wales.

During winter months over some decades Cyril used his vast collection of photographic slides to illustrate his "Slide Shows", which helped with raising funds for the Chapel and many other local organisations.

Cyril Dawson shared his love and knowledge of Langley and it's surrounding countryside by writing weekly *"Nature Notes"* for a local newspaper under the title 'Country Lover'. Some of the few published history books about Langley were written and illustrated by Cyril. He received and answered many enquiries about aspects of local history – some of his correspondents lived overseas.

As an artist, Cyril recorded a variety of local scenes, including Langley Chapel, and each year he illustrated his own individual Christmas cards.

13

Graves and Memorials

Graves.

The graveyard outside Langley Chapel might well be the *"smallest in the country"*: there are only four graves and of these one is usually not visible to casual observers.

The most visible graves are for-

Harold PARKINSON, 1887 – 1888 (who died aged 10 months): brother of Rev. G. Parkinson.

Mrs Elizabeth PIMM, 1787 – 1870 (who was 83 years old when she died): a cousin of the local historian Walter B. Smith, of Macclesfield.

John SMITH, died 1836 (at 32 years of age), his wife Ann, who died in 1875 (aged 72 years), and their daughter Lydia, who died in 1868 (when aged 37 years): this John SMITH was probably a cousin to Isaac SMITH, (who was largely responsible for building the first Langley Chapel).

The least-visible grave, near to the Chapel's main gate-way, is generally grassed-over, and is for-

Mrs WHITE: (*no record has been found with any biographical information about Mrs White*).

Stained-glass memorial Windows.

Langley Church has four beautiful stained-glass windows. The identities of the designer and the maker of these windows are no longer known. These Windows were dedicated to the following four Langley residents-

William SMITH (1825 – 1868), a son of Isaac and Elizabeth SMITH, (window above the Main Door).

Mrs Emma Smith WHISTON (who died when aged 37 years, in 1885); she was the wife of William WHISTON.

Mrs Ann PRICHARD (died 1893, aged 72 years): she was a daughter of Isaac and Elizabeth SMITH.

William WHISTON (1838 – 1915): sometime principal of *"William Whiston and Son"*, silk-printers, Langley.

Memorial Plaques.

There are wall-mounted marble plaques to the following-

Isaac SMITH (who died in 1850, aged 60 years): who operated a textile-processing enterprise in Langley, and who made significant contributions to the first Langley Chapel.

Mrs Elizabeth SMITH, *née* FOUNTAIN, (who died in 1833, aged 44 years): wife of Isaac SMITH.

Two children of Isaac and Elizabeth SMITH: Isaac SMITH (who died in 1832, aged 17 years), and his brother John Smith (who died in 1836, aged 12 years).

Mrs Elizabeth FOUNTAIN (who died in 1845, aged 81 years): presumably the mother of Isaac Smith's wife, Elizabeth.

Samuel SMITH (who died in 1849, aged 32 years): a son of Isaac and Elizabeth SMITH, and Elizabeth (died in 1838 aged 17 months), a daughter of Samuel and Ann Smith.

Other tablets inside the Chapel, made from either brass or copper, are in memory of-

Louie BAY (1883 – 1939)
C. Gordon FREEGARD (lost at sea on 3rd Sept. 1941, aged 51 years)
John Thomas MOORE (1846 – 1929)
Mary Alice MOORE (1852 – 1944)
Gertrude Alice MOORE (1874 – 1954)
Thomas Percy NADEN (1880 – 1946)
Arthur PICKFORD (1891 – 1985), *a plaque and a wooden cross were dedicated 28th September, 1986*
Edith Lilian WHISTON (1867 – 1947)
Harold Walter WHISTON (1873 – 1952)
William Hartington WHISTON (1880 – 1938)

War Memorial.

In the porch of the main entrance to the Chapel is a memorial to the ninety-one men who fought in the 1914 – 1918 War. The twelve Langley men who lost their lives, *"their ultimate sacrifice,"* – were-

Pte William Pickford
c.1918

Pte. Charles ASTLE
Sgt. Thomas AVERY
Lieut. William BAY
Pte. Harry CUNDIFF
Pte. Harold GOLDTHORPE
Pte. William HULLEY, MM
Pte. William PICKFORD
Lce-Corp. Fred. ROSE
Act/Sgt. Harold SIMPSON
Pte. Harold WARDLE
Pte. George WARDLE
Sgt. John WHATMOUGH

Mr Harold Whiston, of "William Whiston & Son", presented the memorial to the people of Langley during an impressive ceremony held on 12th November 1919.

Garden of Remembrance.

The Garden of Remembrance was opened in February 1999 following a service of dedication led by Rev. Derrick Bannister.

Memorial stones may be placed in the Garden, and ashes can be scattered or buried. A book of remembrance is kept in the vestry.

14

Links

"It is in the sphere of Christian Unity that John Wesley made perhaps his greatest contribution to the world of the future. In his famous sermon on the Catholic Spirit he made it clear that 'difference in opinions or modes of worship may prevent an entire external union' *yet they should not prevent a unity of love and co-operation in the Christian witness to the world. We cannot think alike on any subject under the sun, for human nature reveals an infinite diversity of mind and heart. But* 'we can all love alike'*, and it is in the sphere of perfect love that all the people can and should unite."*

The first service in which Langley Methodists and Sutton Anglicans worshipped together was in 1840, soon after St. James' Church was opened. Then, between 1863 and 1880, while The Rev. Ebenezer Smith was the Vicar, the Choirs of St. James' and Langley Chapel sang together at each other's Harvest Festivals and Easter Services.

During the latter half of the 19th century some of the manufacturers in Langley paid rents for pews in both the Chapel and St. James', and also gave other forms of financial support to both places of worship. Each Sunday some Langley residents attended the Morning Service at St. James' Church and the Evening Service at the Chapel.

The silk-printer William Whiston of Langley maintained strong links with both the Anglicans and the Methodists. An indication of his attitude is that in 1896 he paid for new bells to be hung in St. James' and in St. Michael's Parish Church, Macclesfield, and also he funded the large extension to Langley Chapel that was opened that year.

In 1965 the Rev. Wesley Penny, Methodist Minister, and the Anglican Vicar Rev. Alan Stout held the first regular United Services combining Langley Chapel and St. James' Church, Sutton, when the congregations joined together to celebrate long-established Christian events including Easter and Christmas and also Harvest Festival.

Through these links, Methodists and Anglicans have become more aware of the traditions and practices of each other's Church.

The Langley Institute (now the Village Hall) and the Chapel are only 50-yards apart, yet they serve very different community needs.

When William Whiston built the Institute in 1883, he stated that he wanted a building that would complement the Chapel, to serve the needs and interests of all the villagers; he saw the requirement for rooms, outside the Chapel, suitable for club meetings, entertainments and recreation purposes as well as for lectures that would *"... sharpen a man's intelligence...".*

Langley Institute (Village Hall) 1947

An extension added to the Institute was opened to commemorate the Coronation of George V in 1911.

During the 120 years of its existence the Institute has been used for a variety of purposes. Often it has been used in conjunction with Chapel activities that could not be held on the Chapel premises, including the following types of events –

> (a) when alcohol might be consumed or gambling take place such as during parties, whist drives, bingo and billiards competitions;

> (b) when some members of an organisation were not Chapel attendees as, for example, the Mothers' Committee during the 1970s, and

> (c) large community activities, supported by Chapel members, such as:

the Annual Fete; the Macclesfield Carnival Float Competition, and Queen Elizabeth's 50th Jubilee Celebration.

Fr. Fred Robinson 2003
St.Edward's Church

Rev. E. W 'Taffy' Davies
2003 St James' Church

Throughout much of their history, Langley Methodists have enjoyed friendly relationships and contacts with many if not all the other Churches in the district including St. James' Church, Sutton Lane Ends, and St. Edward's Church, Macclesfield, with whom there are shared ecumenical prayer meetings and joint Lent meetings. During Lent the three Churches meet over a number of weeks to discuss relevant topics. In 2003 the topic was the proposed Covenant between the Methodist and Anglican Churches.

Rev. Derrick M Bannister 2003
Langley Methodist Church

Langley is also represented at the meetings of Churches Together in Macclesfield (CTM), which brings together members of most of the Christian Churches in Macclesfield and the surrounding area. One of the achievements of CTM was the opening in 2001 of the "Just Drop In" Centre in Chestergate, Macclesfield. This Centre offers information and advice for people aged between 12 and 25 years of age. Other links to church work beyond Methodism include donations to the work of Christian Aid (mainly for overseas work), and support of Tearfund (which sponsors young people overseas).

Pavicevic Family
Vrbas 2001

In 2003 members of the Langley Methodist Church were attempting to establish links with members of the Methodist Church in Vrbas, Yugoslavia. The photograph shows Vladimir and Piroska Pavicevic at the confirmation of their grand-daughter.

These links and bonds have not been at the expense of any one: each Church has retained its own approaches to worship, music and organisation.

Rev. Stanley Webb
& Catherine Webb c.1990

In November, 1990, the Rev. Stanley Webb wrote about the 150th Anniversary Service held at St. James', Sutton. Langley Methodists derived great joy from taking part in that Service and in sharing with the informal, family gathering afterwards. The following is an extract from the Rev. Webb's article about that Service in *"Langley News"* –

"To me the real enjoyment came from the fact that we could all feel so much at home – all evidence of the links that have strengthened and grown over the years between our churches. We hope to be together again for the first Sunday in Advent (December 2nd) when Father Michael Cupit from St. Edward's will be the preacher at the United Advent Service in Langley Methodist Chapel.

Some still feel worried about growing friendship between the Churches. 'Shan't we lose our own identity?', 'We don't all want to worship in the same way', 'We all have things to treasure' – all these points are true. It would be a very sad day if those differences which make up such a rich variety were to disappear. They are part of our inheritance and I think that there is a real place for our different approaches to worship or to music or to the ways in which we organise ourselves – as long as none of these things divide us or cloud the fact that we are all Christians, united in our belief in God and in our search to follow in the way of Jesus.

The beginning of this month sees the celebration of the Festival of All Saints. What a rich variety of people there have been down the centuries who we have recognised as great examples and leaders. They came from a wealth of countries and backgrounds – young, old, rich, poor, gifted, simple in the very best sense of that word – all sharing through their lives the love of God, and yet using to the full the different gifts that God had entrusted to them.

We see in our own children a vast variety of approaches to life. They are like us in some ways but they have their own likes and dislikes too – they have grown up together – yet have their own clear views which may be miles apart, but sincerely held. Yet when we have looked at all the differences – they are still our own children – part of a Family. The challenge for any family is to go on loving – go on growing in understanding of each other as the years pass – seeing that all the outward differences are not as important as the ties of love that can bind us together. It is the same with the Church. Slowly, patiently, God is guiding us to see our unity – our oneness in His love and concern for each other, our concern for all people in need, will be a help and an example to others.

What a challenge!"

Appendix A

Additions and Renovations

Financial commitment by the congregation has been essential ever since 1858 to keep the Methodist buildings in Langley structurally sound, suitable for their purposes, attractive – and comfortable. To supplement weekly offerings, numerous social functions have been organised. These include: Bazaars, Sales of Work, Fetes, Concerts, Garden Parties, Slide Shows, Talks and other activities. In addition, Arthur Pickford started the Remembrance Fund. All of the monies raised through this initiative are set aside to help pay for the upkeep and improvement of the premises. Generous legacies have also helped to keep the Chapel in good repair and suitable for the many needs of the congregation and of the wider community.

During the past 145 years (1858 – 2003) some of the main changes made to, and within, the second Langley Chapel have been-

1862: Extra heating pipes installed.

1870: Harmonium acquired.

1881: Roof repairs; painting; new carpets (costing £206). Second floor added above the long room. New rostrum table and chairs. Gift of a font. Provision of the Ten Commandments board.

1884: Organ installed (£220).

1885: Window installed in memory of Emma Smith Whiston, the first wife of William Whiston.

1892: Window installed in memory of William Smith, son of Isaac Smith.

1893: Window installed in memory of Mrs Ann Prichard, daughter of Isaac Smith.

1896: Two storey extension and gable; a new external door, and a new vestry.

1905: Connection to water pipe from a spring on Tegg's Nose (£8).

1911: Sunday School extension; new kitchen, and a basement.

1919: Copper memorial plaque to the Langley men who served in World War I.

1923: Electric lighting installed. Coloured glass, to replace ribbed glass.

1924: Window installed to the memory of William Whiston.

1927: New coke-fuelled boiler installed, to replace the original coke-fuelled boiler.

1939: Painting and redecoration.

1949: Gas-fired boiler (to replace the 22-year-old solid fuel unit); Red carpet (to replace coconut matting).

1953: General repairs and redecoration (£1,200).

1958: New toilets, and enlargement of the kitchen.

1960: Addition of car park (on land gifted by William Eric Whiston).

1963: Roof reslated.

1965: External painting.

1971: Repairs to damage caused by dry rot to the Chapel and the Sunday School; Oil-fired boiler installed.

1980: False ceiling fitted to the schoolroom (£947), Introduction of microphone and loud speakers within the Chapel.

1983: Gas boiler, replacement for oil-fired unit (£1,600).

1986: Rewiring of Chapel, and extra lighting (£926).

1989: Car park asphalted (£2,000).

1991: Installation of a new "loop" audio system (£2,128).

1992: The Makin Fanfare Digital Computer Organ replaced the pipe organ (£16,500).

1994: Repairs of areas damaged by wet- and dry-rot (£2,500).

1995: New piano (£2,400).

1997: Garden of Remembrance created and planted (£2,544).

1999: Major extension, alterations and redecorations to the Chapel premises (£45,000 funded by Landfill Tax Grant).

1999: Dedication of the Garden of Remembrance.

2001: Linked smoke alarms fitted. Church sign over entrance gate and unity sign on wall; Replacement of windows in schoolroom and upstairs room (£11,000); Replacement of gutters and downspouts (£3,800).

2002: Outside painting (£1,700).

2003: Replacement of Makin Organ following failure of computer chip.

Appendix B

Trustees

Trustees of (*the first*) Wesleyan Chapel, on 19th May, 1838-

Name	Residence	Occupation
Joshua THORNLEY	Macclesfield	Grocer
James SARGENT	Macclesfield	*Draper*
Thomas BROCKLEHURST	Macclesfield	*Shoemaker*
Finney BOWERS	Macclesfield	*Corn-factor*
Thomas COOPER	*Winshaw Farm,* Sutton	*Farmer*
William MORLEY	Langley	*Grocer*
David HOLLAND	Macclesfield	*Silk Throwster*
John Wright SMALLWOOD	Macclesfield	*Druggist*
John CLULOW	Macclesfield	*Draper*
Ralph BAILEY	Langley	*Grocer*
Joseph Smith BAILEY	Meg Lane	*Farmer*
William HUMPHREYS	Meg Lane	Farmer
John BONSALL	Hurdsfield	*Grocer*

Trustees of (*the second*) Langley Chapel 1858-

Langley	Macclesfield	Meg Lane
John ALLEN	Thomas BROCKLEHURST	William HUMPHREYS
John BAILEY		
Jos. L. BAILEY	Thomas COOPER	
Jno CLULOW	David HOLLAND	
Ralph STEELE	James SARGENT	
Thomas WARDLE	Jno W. SMALLWOOD	

Trustees appointed 24th May, 1858-

Langley	Macclesfield	Meg Lane
William SMITH	Rev. W. BRAILSFORD	William HUMPHREYS
Ralph STEELE	David HOLLAND	
John BAILEY	J. ATKIN	
Thomas WARDLE	H. SMALLWOOD.	

Trustees appointed 24th May, 1882-

Names	
Rev. John Samuel JONES	William WHISTON
Ralph STEELE	John BAILEY
Thomas WARDLE	Thomas COOPER
William Isaac Bradbury SMITH	Edwin Goodwin BALL
Joseph STEELE	William WARREN
William POOL	John BROADHEAD
John Thomas MOORE	Abraham Knowles BERESFORD

Trustees in 1884-

Langley	Macclesfield
John BAILEY	A. K. BERISFORD
Edwin G. BALL	Jno BROADHEAD.
John Thomas MOORE	
R. W. POOL	
Joseph STEELE	
Thomas WARDLE	
William WARREN	
William WHISTON.	

Trustees, as revised in December 1905-

Existing Trustees: 5, inc. 4 from Langley	New appointees: 3 from Langley &/or district	New appointees: 5 from Macclesfield
K. BERISFORD bank manager Alderley Edge.	John MASON farmer "Higher Ridgegate Farm" Sutton.	John CLAYTON builder.
John Thomas MOORE chair manufacturer.	Frederick MILLWARD silk printer.	William HULME silk dyer.
Joseph STEELE mill manager.	Herbert WARREN silk printer.	Wilfred PROCTOR leather factor.
William WARREN farmer.		Frederick WADSWORTH solicitor.
William WHISTON silk printer.		Reginald WEAVER commercial traveller.

The Trust was reformed in 1924, 1937, 1953 and in 1973.

The 1973 Trustees were-

Trustees appointed in 1974-

Appendix C

Timeline

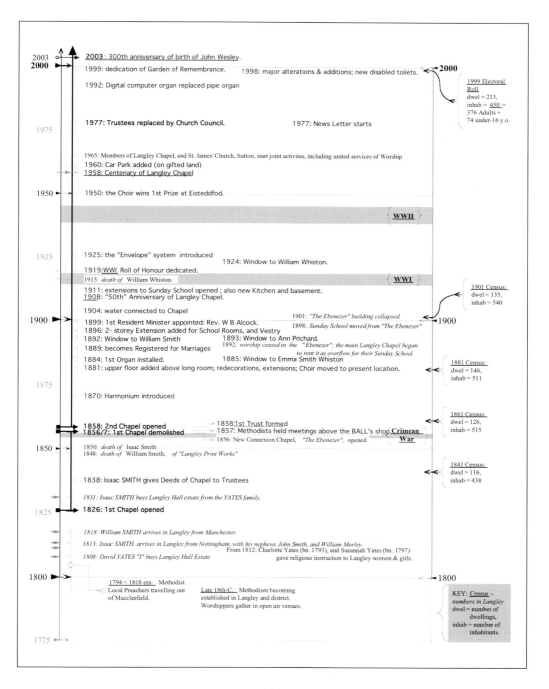

2003
2000 — 2003 : 300th anniversary of birth of John Wesley.
1999: dedication of Garden of Remembrance.   1998: major alterations & additions; new disabled toilets. ◄ **2000**

1992: Digital computer organ replaced pipe organ

1999 Electoral
Roll
dwel = 213,
inhab = 450 =
376 Adults +
74 under-16 y.o.

1977: Trustees replaced by Church Council.   1977: News Letter starts

1975

1965: Members of Langley Chapel, and St. James' Church, Sutton, start joint activites, including united services of Worship
1960: Car Park added (on gifted land)
1958: Centenary of Langley Chapel

1950 — 1950: the Choir wins 1st Prize at Eisteddfod.

WWII

1925 — 1925: the "Envelope" system introduced
1924: Window to William Whiston.
1919:WWI Roll of Honour dedicated.
1915: *death of* William Whiston.   **WWI**
1911: extensions to Sunday School opened ; also new Kitchen and basement.
1908: "50th" Anniversary of Langley Chapel.

1901 Census:
dwel = 135,
inhab = 540

1904: water connected to Chapel   1901: *"The Ebenezer" building collapsed.*
1900 — 1899: 1st Resident Minister appointed: Rev. W B Alcock.   1898: *Sunday School moved from "The Ebenezer"* ◄ **1900**
1896: 2- storey Extension added for School Rooms, and Vestry
1892: Window to William Smith   1893: Window to Ann Prichard.
                                  1892: *worship ceased in the   "Ebenezer"; the main Langley Chapel began*
1889: becomes Registered for Marriages   *to rent it as overflow for their Sunday School.*
1884: 1st Organ installed.   1885: Window to Emma Smith Whiston
1881: upper floor added above long room; redecorations, extensions; Choir moved to present location.

1881 Census:
dwel = 146,
inhab = 511

1875

1870: Harmonium introduced

1861 Census:
dwel = 126,
inhab = 515

1858: 2nd Chapel opened   1858:1st Trust formed
1856/7: 1st Chapel demolished   1857: Methodists held meetings above the BALL's shop **Crimean**
                                     1856: New Connexion Chapel, *"The Ebenezer",* opened.   **War**
1850 — 1850: *death of* Isaac Smith
1848: *death of* William Smith,   *of "Langley Print Works"*

1841 Census:
dwel = 116,
inhab = 438

1838: Isaac SMITH gives Deeds of Chapel to Trustees

1831: Isaac SMITH buys Langley Hall estate from the YATES family.
1825 — **1826: 1st Chapel opened**

1818: William SMITH arrives in Langley from Manchester.

1813: Isaac SMITH arrives in Langley from Nottingham, with his nephews John Smith, and William Morley.
                                  From 1812: Charlotte Yates (bn. 1793), and Susannah Yates (bn. 1797)
1808: David YATES "I" buys Langley Hall Estate   *gave religious instruction to Langley women & girls.*

1800 ►   ◄ **1800**
1794 < 1818 era: Methodist
Local Preachers travelling out   Late 18th-C.: Methodism becoming
of Macclesfield.   established in Langley and district.
                    Worshippers gather in open air venues.

KEY: Census -
numbers in Langley
dwel = number of
    dwellings,
inhab = number of
    inhabitants.

1775

Appendix D

Langley Church Office Holders

Office	Holder
Minister	Rev D Bannister
Church Stewards	Mr D Lockett
	Mr D Bullock
	Mrs B Chapman
	Mr D Potts
	Mr D Sitch
	Mrs J Lewis
Church Secretary	Mr A J Chapman
Church Treasurer	Mr P Wardle
Remembrance Fund	Mrs A Ashton
Gift Aid Secretary	Mr A Lewis
Property Secretary	Mr D Bullock
Pastoral Secretary	Mr D Sitch
Overseas Missions	Mr A Lewis
JMA Secretary	Mrs N Rose
Women's Network	Mrs M Lockett

Office	Holder
Home Missions	Mrs J Lewis
Sunday Club, & Cradle Roll	Mrs K Horrocks & Mrs J Fenton
Prayer Meeting	Mr A Lewis
Flowers	Mrs M McQuinn & Mrs B Jones
Organist	Mr P Wardle
Choir	Mr P Wardle
Music Group	Mr A Spray
Newsletter	Mrs M Wilson
Weekly Notices	Mrs D Wardle Mr A Lewis & Mr D McBryde
Key Holder	Mr N Barber
Christian Aid Secretary	Mr H Jones
Churches Together In Macclesfield	Mrs A Davenport Rev. D Bannister
Tearfund	Mrs R Bullock
Room Bookings	Mrs D Wardle
Archivist	Mrs T Whiston

Church Council

Minister	Rev. Derrick Bannister
Secretary	Alan Chapman
Treasurer	Philip Wardle
Senior Steward	Derek Lockett
Steward	David Bullock
Steward	Brenda Chapman
Steward	David Potts
Steward	Dennis Sitch
Steward	Jenny Lewis
Missions	Tony Lewis
Tearfund	Rowena Bullock
MRDF / Christian Aid	Harry Jones
Womens Network	Margaret Lockett
Remembrance Fund	Mary Ashton
Sunday Club	Roger Fenton
Representatives of the Church Meeting	Dora Wardle Barbara Jones Heather Potts

Church Committees

Property	Mission	Pastoral
Rev. Derrick Bannister	Rev. Derrick Bannister	Rev. Derrick Bannister
Norman Barber	Rowena Bullock	Marion Barlow
David Bullock *	Jenny Lewis	Brenda Berry
Roger Danby	Tony Lewis *	Rowena Bullock
Ron Deegan		Alan & Brenda Chapman
Harry Jones	**Young People**	Jean Hinds
Jenny Lewis	Rev. Derrick Bannister	Jenny Lewis
Derek Lockett	Julia Fenton	Peter & Eileen Simons
David Potts	Karen Horrocks	Dennis Sitch *
Dora Wardle	Jenny Lewis *	
Philip Wardle	Debbie White	
Thelma Whiston		
		* indicates the person responsible for convening the committee.
Worship	**Budget**	
Rev. Derrick Bannister	David Bullock	
Alan Chapman	Alan Chapman *	
Derek Lockett *	Derek Lockett	
Dennis Sitch	Dennis Sitch	
Dora Wardle	Philip Wardle	
Philip Wardle		

Appendix E

Macclesfield Circuit Plan 2003

THE METHODIST CHURCH

MACCLESFIELD CIRCUIT

Plan of Appointments (19/24)

JANUARY-MARCH 2003

(213)

Ministers

	Tel.
Rev. MARK BROADHURST 23, Marlborough Drive, Tytherington, SK10 2JY	426051
Rev. DERRICK M. BANNISTER 11, Atholl Close, SK10 3QB	424361
Rev. RUTH JACKSON 2, Moss Brow, Bollington, SK10 5HH	572259

Supernumerary Ministers

	Tel.
Rev. HOWARD BOOTH 102a, Gawsworth Road, SK11 8UE	426002
Rev. STANLEY JOHNSON 2, Kenilworth Road, SK11 8PE	500237
Rev. FRANK BISHOP 34, Moss Lane, SK11 7TT	433239
Rev. SHEILA BISHOP 34, Moss Lane, SK11 7TT	433239
Rev. RICHARD JACKSON 42, Drummond Way, SK10 4XJ	268622

Chairman of the District

	Tel.
Rev. DAVID F. WILLIE 15, Woodlands Road, Handforth, Wilmslow, SK9 3AW	523480

Circuit Stewards

	Tel.
Mr. GRAHAM JONES 2, The Paddock, Prestbury, SK10 4DB	828654
Mr. TONY LEWIS Tolletts House, Leek Old Road, Sutton, SK11 0HZ	01260 252258
Mr. DON RISELEY 41, Park Mount Drive, SK11 8NS	428358

Price 20p

LOCAL PREACHERS

All addresses Macclesfield unless otherwise stated

* Indicates unable to take appointments.

Unless otherwise stated Telephone (01625)

			Tel.
1953	Mr. K. Ball, 22 Cherryfields Road, Broken Cross, SK11 8RF		425150
1953	Mr. M. Wardlow, H.M.I., 9 Pool End Close, Tytherington. SK10 2JX		423574
1957*	Mr. C. Harlington. 44 Cedar Way, Bollington, SK10 5NS		575462
1958	Mr. I.J.ea, The Oaks, Shellow Lane, North Rode, CW12 2NX	01260	223255
1960	Mr. R. Wrigley, 24 Irwell Rise, Bollington, SK10 5YE		572606
1965	Mrs. F. Gorton, 9 Sandringham Road, SK10 1QB		424180
1965	Mrs. A. Fielding, 135a, Whirley Road, SK10 3JL		428376
1965	Mr. J.M. Burgess, H.M.I., 10, Fir Close, Poynton, Stockport, SK12 1PD		875322
1968	Mrs. C. Broadhurst 23, Marlborough Drive, SK10 2JY		426051
1970	Dr. R. Bolton, 12 Ashfield Drive, SK10 3DQ		420127
1973*	Mrs. C. Harlington, 44 Cedar Way, Bollington, SK10 5NS		575462
1977	Mrs. L Eardley, 35, Sandringham Road, SK10 1QB		420559
1978	Mr. M. Lovatt, 11, Crown Street West, SK11 8EG		435266
1979	Mr. J. Bird, 13, Cherryfields Road, Broken Cross, SK11 8RF		429022
1980*	Mr. R. Pemberton, 19 Gawsworth Road, SK11 8UE		611866
1984	Mrs. D. Chesterman, 159, Woodford Road, Bramhall, Stockport, SK7 1QD	0161	439 7926
1993	Mrs. H. Morrow, 48 Arlington Drive, SK11 8QL		427537
1997	Mrs. S. Walker, 14 High Tree Drive, Henbury, SK11 9PD		427977
2001	Mr. M. Wakelin, 21, Springbank, Bollington, SK10 5LQ		574352

ON TRIAL

	Tel.
Mrs. L. Hall, 9, Holcombe Drive, SK10 2UU	615918
Mr. W. Nightingale, 14, Cheveley Close, SK10 2UB	431191
Mr. S. Oliver, 1 Moorlands Close, SK10 2TL	421046

STUDENT MINISTER

	Tel.
Mrs. J. Bennett, 31, Lord Street, SK11 6SY	503105

VISITING PREACHERS

Mrs. G. Dascombe, 15, Poise Brook Drive, Stockport, Cheshire. SK2 5JG 0161 456 8959

Mr. G. Heapy, 67 Bedford Avenue, Shaw, Oldham, Lancs., OL2 7DR   01706 844242

Rev. G. Newell, 49, Buxton Road, Aylsham, Norwich, Norfolk, NR11 6UB 01263 732102

Prof. J. Turner, 13 Firswood Mount, Gatley, Cheadle, Cheshire, SK8 4JY   0161 283 8429

JANUARY / FEBRUARY / MARCH

	JANUARY				FEBRUARY				MARCH				
	5 (Covenant)	12	19	26	2	9	16 (Education)	23	2	9	16	23	30 (Mothering)
READINGS	Jer 31:7-14; Eph 1:3-14; John 1:10-18	Gen 1:1-5; Acts 19:1-7; Mark 1:4-11	1 Sam 3:1-10; 1 Cor 6:12-20; John 1:43-51	Jonah 3:1-5,10; 1 Cor 7:29-31; Mark 1:14-20	Deut 8:15-20; 1 Cor 8:1-13; Mark 1:21-28	Is 40:21-31; 1 Cor 9:16-23; Mark 1:29-39	2 Kings 5:1-14; 1 Cor 9:24-27; Mark 1:40-45	Is 43:18-25; 2 Cor 1:18-22; Mark 2:1-12	2 Kings 2:1-12; 2 Cor 4:3-6; Mark 9:2-9	Gen 9:8-17; 1 Peter 3:18-22; Mark 1:9-15	Gen 17:1-7; Rom 4:13-15; Mark 8:31-38	Exod 20:1-17; 1 Cor 1:18-25; John 2:13-22	Numb 21:4-9; Eph 2:1-10; John 3:14-21
BOLLINGTON (79) 10.30 / 6.30	Jackson CS	F.Bishop	Broadhurst	Johnson	Jackson S	S.Bishop	Worship Group	Gorton	Jackson S	Bannister G	C.Broadhurst	Wakelin	Eardley
BROKEN CROSS (74) 9.00 / 10.30 / 6.30	Bannister CS	Willie	Bannister P / At URC	Booth S / Bird	Bannister S	Bannister S / Bouon	Bannister P / Johnson	Eardley	Bannister S	Bannister S / Wakelin	Bannister P / Bannister SH	Booth	Jackson LD
GAWSWORTH (41) 10.30 / 6.30	F&S Bishop CS / S.Bishop	S.Bishop	S.Bishop P	Burgess	S.Bishop P	F.Bishop P	Oliver	Johnson	F.Bishop S	Ball	S.Bishop P	C.Broadhurst	S.Bishop
HIGHER HURDSFIELD (6) 2.30	Broadhurst S			Chesterman					Broadhurst				
LANGLEY (78) 10.30 / 6.30	Johnson / Bannister S	Bannister CS / Willie at St. James	Hall / At URC	Bannister / Lovatt	F.Bishop / Booth S	Bannister S / Morrow	Bird / Bannister	Bannister / Eardley	Booth / Bannister S	Jackson S / Wardlow	Broadhurst / Fielding	Bannister / No Service	Wardlow / Chesterman
MACCLESFIELD (204) 10.30 / 3.00 / 6.30	Broadhurst F / Broadhurst CS	Broadhurst CS	Johnson Trinity / At URC	Broadhurst S / Jackson CS	Booth	Broadhurst F	Broadhurst S / Jackson	Lovatt Trinity	Broadhurst F	Broadhurst	Johnson HM	Broadhurst S	Broadhurst Trinity
OVER ALDERLEY (17) 10.30	Chesterman	Fielding	No Service Birtles	Jackson CS	Turner	Johnson	Jackson	Nightingale	Gorton	Bolton	Jackson S	Oliver	Morrow
PRESTBURY (60) 10.30 / 6.45	Booth / Jackson S	Jackson F / Walker	Jackson CS / At URC	Bolton / Jackson US	Dascombe / S.Bishop	Jackson F / Nightingale	Burgess / Jackson S	Broadhurst / Morrow	Hall / Booth SH	Newell F / Newell	L.A. / Bird	Jackson S / Booth	F.Bishop / Jackson S
WALKER BARN (12) 6.30	Broadhurst CS	Booth	Bird	Johnson	Wakelin	Hall	Lovatt	Broadhurst	S.Bishop	Booth S	Broadhurst	Nightingale	Broadhurst
WHITELEY GREEN (8) 2.30 / 6.30	Morrow	Jackson CS	Gorton	Oliver	Fielding	Jackson	Chesterman	Eardley	Wardlow	Burgess	F.Bishop	Jackson S	Hall

C Carols: CA Church Anniversary: Ch Choir Anniversary: CR Cradle Roll: CS Covenant: CT Christingle: F Family Service: FS Flower Service: G Guild: H Healing: HF Harvest Festival: HM Home Missions: LA Local Arrangements: LP Local Preachers' LS Ladies' Sunday: OM Overseas Missions: P Parade: PC Parish Church: PP Prayer and Praise: S Holy Communion: SSA Sunday School Anniversary: T Toy Service: US United Service: Y Young People's Service

Total Circuit Membership 579

LOCAL CHURCH CONTACT PERSONS

Bollington	Mrs. P. Burgess, 10, Fir Close, Poynton, Stockport, SK12 1PD	875322
Broken Cross	Mrs. C. Deegan, 285 Chester Road, SK11 8RA	429581
Gawsworth	Mrs. M. Parkin, 10, Fairfield Close, Gawsworth, SK11 9RX	420843
Higher Hurdsfield	Mrs. A. Wheelton, 1, Hillside Court, Hillside Drive, SK10 2QD	424376
Langley	Mr. D. Lockett, 23, Thistleton Close, SK11 8BE	423422
Macclesfield	Prof. J. Healy, 6, Bittern Grove, SK10 3QP	434326
Over Alderley	Mr. A. Coppock, Hurlbutts, Prestbury Road, Over Alderley, SK10 4UQ	583978
Prestbury	Mrs. J. Pritchard, 30, Roan Court, Buxton Road, SK11 7AQ	420310
Walker Barn	Mr. W. Dean, Hindslough Farm, Buxton Road, Macclesfield Forest, SK11 0AR	01260 252391
Whiteley Green	Mrs. B. Swain, 13, The Crescent, Mottram St. Andrew, SK10 4QW	586490

CIRCUIT EVENTS

Saturday, 18th January 9.30am to 12.00 midday at Prestbury
An opportunity to learn about the proposed Covenant between Anglicans and Methodists- all welcome.

Sunday 19th January, 6.30pm Ecumenical Service at Macclesfield United Reformed Church, Park Green

Monday 3rd March, 7.45pm Circuit Meeting at Langley

Thursday, 6th March at 7.45pm Local Preachers' Meeting at Macclesfield

NEXT PLAN DATES BY 19th JANUARY, PLEASE

Bibliography

AUTHOR	TITLE	PUBLISHER
ALCOCK, Joan P.,	*Methodism in Congleton*	Heads, Congleton, 1967
BALL, Ken,	*Methodism in Gawsworth, 1770 - 1945*	[private publication], 1993
DAVIES, C. Stella (editor),	*A History of Macclesfield*	The University Press, Manchester, 1961
DAWSON, Cyril,	*Langley, a History*	Langley Teachers Centre, 1985
DAWSON, Cyril,	*Methodism in Langley*	[private publication], 1958
DINNIS, Alan,	*St. James Church, Sutton*	Franklyn Press Ltd, 1990
EDWARDS, W. Le Cato,	*Epworth…the home of the Wesleys*	
LONGDEN, George,	*The Industrial Revolution*	Macclesfield & Vale Royal Groundwork Trust, 1988
SMITH, Rev. Benjamin,	*Methodism in Macclesfield*	London Wesleyan Conference Office 1895
SMITH, Winifred P. MBE,	*Frank's Girl*	Pentland Press Ltd, 1994
WHISTON, Harold W.,	*Langley*	Times Printing Works, Macclesfield, 1947
WHOMSLEY, Dennis,	*Methodism in Macclesfield*	[private publication]

Sources

Archives of Langley Chapel (including photographs and illustrations)	Langley
Whiston Family Papers (including photographs and illustrations)	Macclesfield
Cheshire Records Office	Chester
John Rylands Library	Manchester
Macclesfield Library	Macclesfield
General Board of Global Ministries United Methodist Church	USA
www.methodist.org.uk/welcome/history.htm.	UK
Macclesfield Silk Museums	Macclesfield

Photographs and Illustrations

Index